Cambridge Elements

Elements in Eighteenth-Century Connections
edited by
Eve Tavor Bannet
University of Oklahoma
Markman Ellis
Queen Mary University of London

RESTORATION ACTING AND OTHER BUSINESS

The Lives of Henry Harris

David Roberts
Birmingham City University

Shaftesbury Road, Cambridge CB2 8EA, United Kingdom

One Liberty Plaza, 20th Floor, New York, NY 10006, USA

477 Williamstown Road, Port Melbourne, VIC 3207, Australia

314–321, 3rd Floor, Plot 3, Splendor Forum, Jasola District Centre, New Delhi – 110025, India

103 Penang Road, #05–06/07, Visioncrest Commercial, Singapore 238467

Cambridge University Press is part of Cambridge University Press & Assessment, a department of the University of Cambridge.

We share the University's mission to contribute to society through the pursuit of education, learning and research at the highest international levels of excellence.

www.cambridge.org
Information on this title: www.cambridge.org/9781009542180

DOI: 10.1017/9781009542197

© David Roberts 2025

This publication is in copyright. Subject to statutory exception and to the provisions of relevant collective licensing agreements, no reproduction of any part may take place without the written permission of Cambridge University Press & Assessment.

When citing this work, please include a reference to the DOI 10.1017/9781009542197

First published 2025

A catalogue record for this publication is available from the British Library

ISBN 978-1-009-54218-0 Hardback
ISBN 978-1-009-54216-6 Paperback
ISSN 2632-5578 (online)
ISSN 2632-556X (print)

Cambridge University Press & Assessment has no responsibility for the persistence or accuracy of URLs for external or third-party internet websites referred to in this publication and does not guarantee that any content on such websites is, or will remain, accurate or appropriate.

For EU product safety concerns, contact us at Calle de José Abascal, 56, 1°, 28003 Madrid, Spain, or email eugpsr@cambridge.org

Restoration Acting and Other Business

The Lives of Henry Harris

Elements in Eighteenth-Century Connections

DOI: 10.1017/9781009542197
First published online: December 2025

David Roberts
Birmingham City University
Author for correspondence: David Roberts, david.roberts@bcu.ac.uk

Abstract: How did actors of the late seventeenth century supplement their earnings? And what were the relationships between their other business and their acting? This Element focuses on the diverse career of Henry Harris, a leading member of the Duke's Company between 1661 and 1682, and co-manager of the company for a decade. A skilled engraver, Harris also held appointments at the Royal Mint and as Yeoman of the Revels at court, all against the background of a fragmented private life. Drawing on recently discovered manuscript material, this is the first full-length study of a major performer of the Restoration period.

This Element also has a video abstract: www.cambridge.org/EECC-Roberts_abstract

Keywords: Restoration theatre, history of acting, celebrity studies, gender studies, theatre economics

© David Roberts 2025

ISBNs: 9781009542180 (HB), 9781009542166 (PB), 9781009542197 (OC)
ISSNs: 2632-5578 (online), 2632-556X (print)

Contents

1 The Portfolio Profession — 1

2 Harris Family Matters — 8

3 In the Duke's Company — 11

4 Petitioning for Seals — 27

5 Managing — 36

6 Marital Woes — 43

7 Last Years — 51

List of Abbreviations of Frequently Cited Sources — 60

Appendix: A Checklist of Henry Harris's Known Roles — 61

Bibliography — 64

1 The Portfolio Profession

Acting is a famously precarious profession, yet we know surprisingly little about the long history of its precarity. What else actors of the past did to make ends meet, and how their other employment related to their acting, are questions whose answers sit largely obscured by patchy evidence. *Restoration Acting and Other Business* uncovers fresh trails of evidence that tell a compelling, multi-track story about the situation of actors in late seventeenth-century London. It is primarily the story of a man who both typified the economic strains of his profession and managed to defy their odds, thanks to an unusual combination of acquired skills, social connections, and personal attributes. That some of those attributes were thoroughly undesirable, and tested during a turbulent private life, further enlivens the tale.

In Restoration London, the actors we know anything about were few in number: between forty and fifty in a given season, and in almost all cases attached to licensed companies running on frantic schedules. Performances on six afternoons a week were preceded by morning rehearsal and followed in some cases by evenings of private study. While the theatrical season typically lasted from September to June or July, coinciding with the terms of the Inns of Court and representing an average total of thirty-five weeks a year, performances might also take place in August, on top of additional commitments for seasons in Oxford or, more frequently, royal command shows at Whitehall in the evening, sometimes directly after an afternoon performance at the public theatre. Estimates of actors' pay in the period suggest what in modern terms would be a modest ratio of junior to senior salaries: specifically a range of £1 to £5 a week.[1] Comparison with current values suggests that translates into the difference between £250 and £1,250 a week, but for acting weeks only, which would mean an annual range of £11,000 to £55,000 in present-day terms – a range that might be said to reach from impossible-to-live-on to just-about-comfortable.[2]

However, the income gap widened when share ownership and managerial roles were taken into account. On 5 November 1660, Sir William Davenant signed an agreement with the ten senior actors of his newly formed Duke's Company. Out of fifteen shares, three were to be retained by Davenant for capital expenditure. Of the remaining twelve, Davenant claimed a further seven

---

[1] *The London Stage Part One. 1660–1700,* ed. William van Lennep (Carbondale and Edwardsville: Southern Illinois University Press, 1963), p.lv. Hereafter referred to as LS1.
[2] In an authoritative study, Robert D. Hume argues that 250 is a reasonable multiplier for translating Restoration period values into modern ones, while admitting the considerable difficulty of drawing comparisons; see his 'The Value of Money in Eighteenth-Century England: Incomes, Prices, Buying Power – and Some Problems in Cultural Economics', *Huntington Library Quarterly* 77.4 (Winter 2014), 373–416.

shares 'to maintain all the women that are to perform' (i.e. in a boarding house attached to the theatre), leaving a half share each to the ten principal actors, who could accordingly draw on daily profits. For a £30 profit that meant £1 per half share. There was a condition: 'they each and every of them shall become bound to the said Sir William Davenant in a bond of £5000'.[3] Entrenching a gender gap, the agreement points to a further concentration of responsibility. Two actors, Thomas Betterton and Thomas Sheppey, are consistently named in surviving documents as though presumptive leaders, with James Nokes occasionally appearing in the same capacity.

Even for those so favoured, the acting profession's precarity was compounded by the number of events that closed theatres and shut off income streams for weeks or months: plague or fire (June 1665 to October 1666), war (June 1667), periods of royal mourning (July and August 1670, January 1685, etc.), not to mention occasional orders arising from the Lord Chamberlain's disapproval of satirical or subversive content, violence, or other kinds of non-compliance with authority. Tempting though it is to draw a line between the shareholders at the top of the income tree and the day labourers below, supplementary employment was a fact of life for just about anyone working in the theatre. But what could an actor do when acting threatened to absorb most of the working day, and for six days a week?

A handful wrote plays, potentially attracting the author's profit that might come from a third performance, plus one-off payments from booksellers for the copy, or royal command appearances.[4] More often, actors had to pursue business beyond the theatre. In the case of the Duke's Company founded by Sir William Davenant in 1660, they came prepared, because Davenant recruited younger actors with trade backgrounds that helped fill the periods when theatres fell silent. Thomas Betterton had trained as a bookseller and maintained an interest in the business.[5] When he played Hamlet in 1661, his Claudius was Thomas Lillieston, a former weaver from Holborn who grew up in the same parish as the First Gravedigger, Cave Underhill, son of a cloth worker. James and Robert Nokes owned a knick-knack shop that was still going in 1680; when the comedian Anthony Leigh joined the company in the early 1670s he brought

---

[3] Articles of agreement between Davenant and the Duke's Company actors, 5 November 1660, reproduced in David Thomas and Arnold Hare, eds., *Restoration and Georgian England 1660–1788* (Cambridge: Cambridge University Press, 1989), pp. 33–35.
[4] On this practice, see Judith Milhous and Robert D. Hume, *The Publication of Plays in London 1660–1800: Playwrights, Publishers and the Market* (London: British Library, 2015), pp. 33–56.
[5] Christine Ferdinand, 'Thomas Betterton's Book-Trade Apprenticeship and the Amazing Careers of His Two Masters, John Holden and John Rhodes, with Some Notes on the Actor's Library', *The Library: The Transactions of the Bibliographical Society* 23.4 (December 2022), pp. 435–57.

skills as a painter.⁶ For graphic ability, no one matched in achievement or opportunism the last actor-shareholder to be recruited, a man described in the agreement as 'of the Citty of London, painter': Henry Harris. So, at least some among what Judith Milhous has described as a 'motley assortment of inexperienced actors' found a way of keeping going with their former trades.⁷ Far from being a distraction, those shadow careers made for the kind of disciplined, entrepreneurial outlook that distinguished them from their counterparts in the King's Company, whose two principal actors, Charles Hart and Michael Mohun, had fought as officers on the Royalist side in the Civil War and probably received pensions as a result.

No ancillary business is better documented than the shop owned by William and Susanna Mountfort. William joined the Duke's Company in the mid-1670s; Susanna, the King's for its last season before the merger that created the United Company in 1682. Both rose quickly to leading roles in the new company, until William's death. Fatally wounded in December 1692, William Mountfort bequeathed to his wife and daughter an estate that included an 'India shop' selling luxury home ware, the inventory for which has recently been unearthed by Christine Ferdinand.⁸ That document offers insight not just into alternative fields of employment, but the couple's immersion in the trade that came of the nascent project of empire.

The Mountforts' premises were in Norfolk Street, conveniently located between the Strand and the River Thames: handy for deliveries as well as for wealthy customers travelling by boat. Since the house had accommodation for servants, it is reasonable to speculate that the Mountforts had help running the shop. After William's death, it took a team of five appraisers two days to value the contents, which included bedsteads, paintings, books, silver, china, silk, walnut furniture, kitchen and tableware, and a 'Japan table'. The total value was determined to be £1,072 4s 11d (something like £270,000 today). When the parish tax collector called in 1693, he found Susanna had left. She would remarry in 1694, and Ferdinand speculates that she sold off the contents, possibly to Peter Motteux, a playwright and translator who in turn would run his own India shop.⁹

---

⁶ For Nokes and Leigh, see Judith Milhous and Robert D. Hume, 'The Prologue and Epilogue for *Fools Have Fortune; Or, Luck's All*, 1680', *Huntington Library Quarterly* no.43 (1980), 313–21.
⁷ Judith Milhous, *Thomas Betterton and the Management of Lincoln's Inn Fields, 1695–1708* (Carbondale: Southern Illinois University Press, 1979), p. 3.
⁸ Christine Ferdinand, 'Commodities and the Acting Profession: A Newly Discovered Inventory for William and Susanna Mountfort's "India Shop" (1692)', *Huntington Library Quarterly* 86.1 (Spring 2023), 73–109.
⁹ On Motteux, Ferdinand cites *The Spectator*, no.288 (30 January 1712).

The Mountforts' profile as performers (William was apparently a favourite of Queen Mary) doubtless helped with custom.[10] If allusions to gambling in Thomas Southerne's 1693 comedy, *The Maid's Last Prayer*, are any guide, it is possible that the gaming tables listed in the Norfolk Street inventory doubled up as a further commercial attraction; in the play, a character called Siam runs just such a dual operation, combining respectable trade on the street frontage with hustling to the rear. An actor's skills might attract more elevated custom. During the 1690s, Betterton was employed to instruct the not-yet-teenage Sir John Perceval, Earl of Egmont, 'in those Parts of Oratory which consist of Emphasis and Action' (Perceval was already enrolled at a private academy where he learned languages, music, and 'hardy Exercises' including dancing, fencing and fighting with a quarter-staff, presumably deemed essential not just for public life but for his future at Westminster School).[11] Clergymen such as Ralph Bridges also sought Betterton's help, giving substance to Charles Gildon's claim that the actor was an expert in the oratorical skills demanded of all performers, whether on the stage, in the pulpit, or at the bar.[12]

Betterton became wealthy enough to lose a fortune in 1692, when a ship carrying goods from India was seized by the French.[13] His loss is estimated at somewhere between £2000 and £8000 (at the upper end, perhaps £2 m in current values). Investment in imperial trade came with colossal risks as well as benefits. When he died, he left behind at least 600 books, 66 paintings, and 2,500 prints and drawings, all put up for auction at his Russell Street lodgings, with some conceivably drawn from a country residence near Reading. There is evidence of his correspondence with an aristocratic family regarding works of art.[14] James Nokes had also amassed funds on a scale that reflected success beyond as well as within the theatre. His will lists houses near the Middle Temple and in Totteridge (then in the countryside outside London), and a share in the New River Waterworks.[15]

---

[10] On her admiration of William Mountfort as Willmore in Behn's *The Rover*, see Cibber, *Apology*, p. 95.

[11] James Anderson, *A Genealogical History of the House of Yvery*, 2 vols. (London, 1742), II.404.

[12] For Bridges, see Judith Milhous, 'Thomas Betterton', ODNB V.557, citing a letter from the Devonshire MSS; for Gildon, *The Life of Mr Thomas Betterton, the Late Distinguished Tragedian* (London: Robert Gosling, 1710).

[13] Joseph Towers, 'The Life of Dr John Radcliffe', *British Biography*, 10 vols. (Sherborne, 1766–67), VII.256–7.

[14] For the auction catalogue, see Jacob Hooke, *Pinacotheca Bettertonaeana*, ed. David Roberts (London: The Society for Theatre Research, 2013); for Betterton's correspondence, David Roberts, *Thomas Betterton: The Greatest Actor of the Restoration Stage* (Cambridge: Cambridge University Press, 2010), pp. 173–83.

[15] National Archive PROB 11/434/232.

Actresses fared differently. Susanna Mountfort may have had the freedom to dispose of William's goods but in 1695 her second husband, the actor John Verbruggen, received £75 for giving the theatre manager Thomas Skipwith permission to employ her. In addition Verbruggen was to receive '£4 out of every £20 to be divided among the adventurers' (i.e. investors) – on the face of it, a generous deal except for the appended note explaining that 'because a Share produced nothing', Skipwith simply loaned Verbruggen the money. Susanna was promised the same share but given the security that her yearly earnings would not fall below £105 (£26,250 in current values), or £3 per acting week.[16] She may have regretted disposing of the India shop. Share ownership for actresses was a novelty of the 1690s. Until then, they had been salaried at best to the tune of half the rate of leading men. Even the great Elizabeth Barry drew only £2 10s a week to Betterton's £5. Her success on the stage did, however, bring a further innovation in the shape of annual benefit performances, and there is evidence not only that she was comfortable enough to lend others substantial sums of money, but that she owned significant property.[17] Betterton's wife, the actress Mary Saunderson, earned money from training younger actors, but largely when her own career was in decline. An actress's best chance of living well was arguably to give up acting – to allow herself to be taken up, as Moll Davis and Nell Gwyn were, by a wealthy member of the aristocracy, whose intentions were hardly altruistic.[18]

In other words, any actor in the theatre of Restoration London, however successful, was involved in a scramble first for basic levels of comfort, and second for a semblance of luxury, and always via the deployment of different skills. Thomas Skipwith's agreement with John Verbruggen required him not just to act, but to sing and dance, skills that could be turned to account beyond the playhouse.[19] The economics of performance demanded another level of multi-skilling: the ability to use one's talents in whatever field, and in whatever way, was within reach.

A focus on lives beyond the theatre suggests an adjustment to the kind of theatre history that demarcates its business by drawing firm lines around play texts, performances, rehearsals, playing spaces, and their respective economics.[20]

---

[16] Articles of agreement between John Verbruggen and Sir Thomas Skipwith, 10 April 1695, LC 7/3, cited in Allardyce Nicoll, *Restoration Drama 1660-1700*, 3rd ed. (Cambridge: Cambridge University Press, 1940), pp. 344–5.

[17] For Barry's finances, Elizabeth Howe, *The First English Actresses: Women and Drama, 1660–1700* (Cambridge: Cambridge University Press, 1992), pp. 27–30. Her will is in the National Archive, PROB 11/536/276, and lists properties in Newbury and substantial bequests.

[18] See Howe, *The First English Actresses*, pp. 32–36.

[19] In Nicoll, *Restoration Drama 1660-1700*, p. 354.

[20] For example, Robert D. Hume, 'Theatre History, 1660–1800: Aims, Materials, Methodology', in Michael Cordner and Peter Holland, eds., *Players, Playwrights, Playhouses: Investigating Performance, 1660–1800* (New York and Basingstoke: Palgrave Macmillan, 2007), pp. 9–44.

That does not entail a lapse into the kind of gossip mongering and intrusiveness, vicious and otherwise, that characterized a number of early biographies of actors, and in some cases continues to do so.[21] What it does entail is an enlarged understanding first of theatre economics, and second of the social networks and contingencies that in the late seventeenth century created opportunity (or barriers to it) among the acting profession. By professional necessity, actors are radically social beings whose careers are comprehensible only amid a web of connections. Studies of them should therefore explore the potential of what Derrida called biographical 'circumfession' – an act of 'de-centring' that locates the subject in multiple sites of commerce, patronage, law, and entertainment.[22]

Recent research by Christine Ferdinand and Richard Palmer has shown what rich materials await the scholar prepared to hunt for evidence outside the usual boundaries of theatre history. Ferdinand's account of the Mountforts' India Shop draws on a will long hidden among the vast holdings of the UK's National Archive, while Palmer has mined the much less well-known (and far less accessible) records of the Court of Arches at Lambeth Palace. The Court took its name from the church of Sancta Maria de Arcubus (now St Mary-le-Bow, London, its home before the Great Fire). It was the highest ecclesiastical court in the Province of Canterbury, and its remit was broad. Probate, defamation, church property, and the morality of both clergy and laity all lay within its jurisdiction. In no domain was its business more contentious than that of marriage and divorce, records for which reveal in considerable detail the personal affairs of plaintiffs and defendants. Palmer's study of the King's Company actor John Lacy's marital woes concludes, encouragingly, that 'many more discoveries' await researchers into the records of the Court of Arches.[23]

Here, the focus is on the career of a painter, actor, manager, singer, engraver, entrepreneur, and libertine who, for variety of talent, for sheer hustle, and for a willingness to accept the carnage such a life might inflict on personal obligations, embodies what it meant to extract money from Restoration acting and other business. The name of Henry Harris is not a conspicuous one in theatre history compared with his contemporaries Thomas Betterton, Elizabeth Barry, or Anne Bracegirdle. He occupies a corner of my 2010 biography of Betterton, a

---

[21] For example, Cheryl Wanko, *Roles of Authority: Thespian Biography and Celebrity in Eighteenth-Century Britain* (Lubbock: Texas Tech University Press, 2003).

[22] I expand on this argument in 'Writing the Ethical Life: Theatrical Biography and the Case of Thomas Betterton', in Claire Cochrane and Jo Robinson, eds., *Theatre History and Historiography. Ethics, Evidence and Truth* (Basingstoke and New York: Palgrave Macmillan, 2016), pp. 33–47.

[23] For Ferdinand, see earlier, n.8; also Richard Palmer, 'In the Court of Arches: The Private Life of John Lacy, Restoration Actor', *Archives* LVIII.1 (2023), 1–13.

project that set in motion an attempt to imagine Henry Harris in fiction (a work which it is fair to say has not enjoyed a wide readership).[24] For want of evidence at the time, his career before 1661 and after 1681 is thinly represented in the *Biographical Dictionary of Actors*. He makes a fleeting appearance in Joseph Roach's influential study of celebrity, *It*, but as an actor who perforce yielded to Betterton in Pepys's appreciation of Orrery's *Henry V*, even though he played the title role in that play.[25]

The idea of celebrity, the degree to which it is appropriate to describe Harris as one, and indeed whether the term suits Restoration actors in the way some scholars have argued, form a thread through this book.[26] Since Roach's book, it has become routine to view the Restoration period as the birthplace of modern ideas of celebrity: a site where individual profile elides or, depending on who was looking, collides with established social structures. Mark S. Dawson has argued that the abuse heaped on some Restoration performers was a way of controlling the threat they were believed to present to prevailing certainties about social class.[27] Study of Henry Harris's multiple careers shows, by contrast, how deeply implicated actors might be in those very certainties and the networks that maintained them.

Harris's lack of visibility in modern scholarship is partly the effect of his professional adaptability. When a new entry on him was commissioned for the *Oxford Dictionary of National Biography*, the task fell not to a theatre historian but to the foremost chronicler of the Royal Mint, where Harris worked during more than three decades, for some of that time alongside his acting and theatre management commitments. Yet Harris matters precisely because his complex professional life illuminates a hitherto barely examined hinterland of the acting profession in the late seventeenth century. Numerous studies have offered generous insight into the varieties of work Restoration writers had to undertake to secure a living: their often fragile relationships with publishers, their eye for paid opportunity, their dependence on patrons and implication in politics.[28] The many careers of Henry Harris show how the work of actors might also be caught up in the relentlessly hustling commercial environment of Restoration London.

---

[24] Roberts, *Thomas Betterton*, pp. 83–96, and *The Life of Harris the Actor* (Birmingham and Shanghai: Goldword, 2015).

[25] Joseph Roach, *It* (Ann Arbor: The University of Michigan Press, 2007), pp. 228–29.

[26] For a recent essay, see Julia H. Fawcett, 'Celebrity and the Restoration Actress', in Matthew C. Augustine and Steven N. Zwicker, eds., *The Oxford Handbook of Restoration Literature* (Oxford: Oxford University Press, 2025), pp. 155–69.

[27] Mark S. Dawson, *Gentility and the Comic Theatre of Late Stuart London* (Cambridge: Cambridge University Press, 2005).

[28] See, for example, James Anderson Wynn, *John Dryden and His World* (New Haven and London: Yale University Press, 1987); Kerry Downes, *Sir John Vanbrugh: A Biography* (New York: St Martin's Press, 1987); Janet Todd, *Aphra Behn: A Secret Life* (London: Fentum Press, 2017).

He was undoubtedly a creature of his age, in all its contradictions. A libertine, master conversationalist, and player of kings who consorted with the aristocracy, he also frequented sordid taverns, leeched off acquaintances, made risky investments, strove to stave off creditors, and seized any opportunity to turn his skills to account. In his variety he might remind us of Dryden's Zimri, an alias for George Villiers, 2nd Duke of Buckingham:

> A man so various, that he seemed to be
> Not one, but all mankind's epitome ...
> Was everything by starts, and nothing long;
> But in the course of one revolving moon,
> Was chemist, fiddler, statesman, and buffoon.[29]

The difference is that the 'epitome' who was Henry Harris was driven by the harsh economic reality facing all Restoration performers, of whatever distinction. For him, its harshness was accentuated by turbulent domestic circumstances, and in turn alleviated by elite connections and by the very trade background from which he had, with a rapidity typical of his age, spectacularly risen. Did that make him an exceptional case or representative of his age and profession? The answer, surely, is both.

2 Harris Family Matters

Henry Harris's roots lay firmly in trade. For the past two generations at least, his family had been makers, and for John Harris of Adstock in Buckinghamshire, that meant shoes.[30] In 1606 he had a son, christening him Timothy at the nearby village of Great Horwood. Timothy would be apprenticed to the Clothworkers' Company in 1621. The Clothworkers were traditionally last in the order of precedence among the livery companies, behind the Mercers, Grocers, Drapers, Fishmongers, Goldsmiths, Skinners, Merchant Taylors, Haberdashers, Salters, Ironmongers, and Vintners.

Because apprenticeships in the Company were not confined to working with cloth, Timothy Harris acquired skills as a maker of weighing scales, in particular the beams that connect the two pans. His wife Joan had some aptitude in the business as

---

[29] John Dryden, 'Absalom and Achitophel', in *John Dryden. The Oxford Authors*, ed. Keith Walker (Oxford: Oxford University Press, 1987), ll.545–50, p. 192. I am grateful to one of the Press's readers for drawing my attention to this comparison.

[30] Information about Harris's family and that of his future wife is drawn variously from the records of the Court of Arches (Arches E 6/98, E 6/138, Ee 4, ff. 560–562, 581–588, E 6/96, Eee 6 ff. 336–338, 341–345, 397–400, A 13 f. 66r.,B 10/54), from the apprenticeship books of the Clothworkers' Company (CL/C/4, CL/C/3/1/2, CL/D/5/9), and from T. C. Dale, *The Inhabitants of London in 1638* (London, 1931), pp. 79–80. This section draws substantially on Richard and Palmer and David Roberts, 'Harris vs Harris: A Restoration Actor at the Court of Arches', *Huntington Library Quarterly* 87.3 (Autumn 2024), pp. 483–500.

well; in 1658, after Timothy's death, she would be described as a scale-maker who had taken on a new apprentice. At least from 1638, Joan and Timothy lived and traded in the parish of St John Zachary in the east of London, probably down St Anne's Lane (there is proof they were there the following decade). At the eastern end was the church of St John Zachary itself; to the west, a short way up Aldersgate Street, was St Botolph's. Within a stone's throw of the stink of Smithfield and the Town Ditch, and a short walk from Newgate Prison, it was hardly the most attractive part of town. Yet St Anne's Lane was, at least, home to two distinguished names. The royalist poet and clergyman Robert Herrick moved there after being ejected from his Devon living in 1647; in 1659, the composer Henry Purcell was born there.

Timothy and Joan were industrious parents. Their eldest son John, named for his shoemaker grandfather, was one of four young Harrises who would also establish themselves as scale-makers, and one of the ten apprentices Timothy took on between 1630 and 1651. Towards the latter end of that period, Timothy was listed in the apprenticeship records as a blacksmith (1644) as well as a balance maker (1648) and beam maker (1651) – the first of those terms perhaps indicating how circumstances might require the adaptability to embrace less skilled commissions. There is no sign that young John Harris deviated from the trade in which he had been apprenticed. Bound to Timothy in 1644, he gained his freedom a year earlier than usual, in 1650, set up on his own in Rood Lane, and was still going in the late 1670s.

Precisely when his younger brother Henry came into the world is not known. Apprenticed, like his father and brother before him, as a scale-maker, Henry Harris gained his freedom of the Clothworkers' Company in 1654, which suggests a birth year of 1633 or 1634. To grow up around the premises of a scale-maker-cum-blacksmith was to be exposed to the relentless routines, sights, and smells of a trade punctuated by occasional holidays and church attendance. It appears Henry used the craft environment of his boyhood to develop a range of related skills and ambitions. By 1656, when he took on his own apprentice, he was described as a 'seal maker' – an occupation that required a finer degree of graphic and craft skills, and attracted a more elevated clientele. He worked in a neighbourhood to suit, on the Strand, close to the heart of the ever-more fashionable West End.[31]

By then he was married. The parish register of St Botolph Aldersgate shows that on New Year's Eve 1655 Harris married Anne Johnson of Whetstone, Middlesex, but formerly of Loughton, Buckinghamshire. Loughton is only 5 miles from where Harris's father grew up; among Timothy's apprentices in St Anne's Lane were boys

---

[31] See Lawrence Stone, 'The Residential Development of the West End of London in the Seventeenth Century', in Barbara C. Malament, ed., *After the Reformation. Essays in Honour of J.H. Hexter* (Manchester: Manchester University Press, 1980), pp. 167–212.

born in Loughton. If it was not an arranged marriage, there is a suggestion that long-standing family contacts played some part in the union. When Henry Harris took on his own first apprentice, family ties tightened still further: the boy Richard, 'son of Richard Johnson of Whetstone, farmer', was Anne's younger brother. Harris was not the most attentive master. Instead of the customary seven years, Richard's servitude lasted twelve; for eight of those years Harris was preoccupied with his role as a leading actor in the Duke's Company. When Richard finally gained his freedom of the Clothworkers' Company in 1668, he took on his own apprentice.

Anne Harris characterized her father as one of the richest, ablest, and most respected men of his parish: a prosperous dairy farmer supplying meat, cheese and butter to the great markets of London. So wealthy was he, she said, that her dowry ran to somewhere between £1,000 and £1,600. Not only that: her parents helped the young couple set up home in the Strand, paying the initial fee of £40 for the tenancy and even, as the need arose, the rent of £42 a year.[32] Owned by the physician Henry Nisbett, their first home was a substantial property: a shop, parlour, kitchen on the ground floor, a cellar beneath, and nine chambers and garrets above. The place was spacious enough for maids, and even other tenants. Its upper rooms were sublet to the tune of £15 a year.[33] After that, the young couple moved twice: first to Clare Street, near Clare Market in Westminster, and then Scroop's Court, on the north side of Holborn close to the church of St Andrew Holborn. By 1661 a baby daughter had appeared. She was named for her father. Anne would recall taking the infant Henrietta on outings to London's pleasure gardens.[34] But her marriage was already under severe strain.

Seventeen years later, in 1678, Henry and Anne would dispute each other's narratives with entrenched bitterness. Henry could not dispute the existence of the premises in the Strand, or that his brother-in-law and former apprentice Richard worked in the same locale (and perhaps the same house), and as a goldsmith, or that he himself had worked 'as goldsmith or graver or both'.[35] What he did dispute was that he owed his good fortune to his father-in-law. Richard Johnson, he argued, was not a wealthy farmer at all, but a mere market trader who brought meat into London for sale. Local records for Loughton and Whetstone do not settle the argument one way or the other, except that seventeenth-century Whetstone was no more than a hamlet, and therefore a singularly small pond in which to be the big fish of Anne's account.[36] It is hardly implausible either that

---

[32] Records of the Court of Arches, Ee 4 ff. 581r-588v.
[33] National Archives, C10/110/54. The property was owned by the physician Henry Nisbett, whose will mentions the tenancy of Henry Harris (National Archives PROB 11/304/422).
[34] Arches Ee 4 ff. 581r-588v.   [35] Arches Eee 6 f.343r.
[36] 'A. Constable Ltd', in *The Victoria History of the County of Buckinghamshire*, ed. William Page (London, 1927), vol. 4, pp. 395–401. In Samuel Lewis's *A Topographical Dictionary of England*, 7th ed. (London, 1858), Whetstone is recorded as having only 782 inhabitants.

Harris, testifying to a marital court on the back of an acting career that had seen him frequent fashionable coffee houses and consort with royalty, may have felt inclined to look down on mere farmers, however well-heeled. The only one of the Harris boys to reject life as a scale-maker, he had long entertained a finer vision of his future. In any case, he was at pains to assert, Anne's memory was evidently faulty. She could not remember accurately the size of her dowry, and that, Harris argued, was because she was constantly drunk.

One final detail about the Johnsons hints at a double schism Harris opened up – with his own family and with his in-laws – when he embarked on a career as an actor. When Anne made her representations to the Court of Arches, she named as a witness a man of unimpeachable credentials whom she described as a close family friend. Since 1643, the eminent physician Dr Nathan Paget, friend to John Milton and cousin to his third wife, had lived in the Puritan enclave of Coleman Street, five minutes' walk to the east of the Harris home. As censor of the College of Physicians from 1655, Paget had a number of options when it came to getting to work in Warwick Lane, but one of the quickest routes was via St Anne's Lane. If the Johnsons – whether wealthy farmers or mere drovers – shared Paget's Puritan inclinations, they would surely have been horrified to see their son-in-law abandon the steady trade for which his father had dutifully prepared him, in favour of the precarious (and, for many Puritans, sordid) life of the stage.

3 In the Duke's Company

How did a maker of scales and seals come to be an actor? And not just any actor, but a shareholder accorded what Davenant's Articles of Agreement with his ten principal actors describe as 'a portion equal to the highest'?[37] Harris had not been part of a group that had cohered in the risky, semi-legal world of theatre born in 1659 – the group, that is, run by the former bookseller John Rhodes in which the twenty-four-year-old Thomas Betterton had quickly emerged as the leading man. Clearly Harris possessed talents far beyond what could be expected of a recently qualified scale-maker and engraver. In the 1660 agreement with Davenant, his description as 'of the Citty of London, painter' has led some to suppose that he must have been recruited for the contribution he could make to the new vogue for movable, painted scenery.[38] Maybe so, as a sideline, but production staff did not qualify for shareholder status. It is also tempting to

---

[37] Articles of agreement between Davenant and the Duke's Company Actors, 5 November 1660, *Document Register* no.44.
[38] C. E. Challis, 'Henry Harris', *Oxford Dictionary of National Biography*, ed. Lawrence Goldmann, 60 vols (Oxford: Oxford University Press, 2004), vol. 25 p. 427.

think that Harris played some part in Davenant's 1656 staging of his *First Day's Entertainment at Rutland House*, a scenic semi-opera devised to evade prevailing restrictions on public performances. But Harris's name features nowhere in records of that event, although he did take a prominent role when the show was revived in 1661 as *The Siege of Rhodes*. There, he not only had to act out a range of passions. He also had to sing.

The only surviving portrait of Harris suggests further reasons why Davenant recruited him. Around 1664 he was painted by John Greenhill in the role of Cardinal Wolsey, as featured in Shakespeare and Fletcher's *Henry VIII*.[39] With Hampton Court in the background, Harris's Wolsey holds his fateful letter to the Pope, his face lined not with age, tragic cunning or bullish determination, but a kind of anxious ardour. Slim and conventionally handsome, he is a Romeo who has stumbled into the College of Cardinals. So far as we can picture the other members of Davenant's new company, Harris's romantic-lead good looks probably stood out. Betterton had 'an ill figure, being clumsily made, having a great head' and 'a short thick neck'; his strengths in large part stemmed from a vocal technique of extraordinary power and subtlety.[40] Nokes was built for clown roles, Underhill where bulk was an asset, and Lillieston where years were required. Harris's versatility and youthful presence made him an obvious fit.

His first season with the Duke's Company, lasting from June 1661 at least until May 1662, was one of his busiest. Records (admittedly imperfect) indicate seven new roles. The first was probably on 28 June 1661, as the Sicilian Duke, Alphonso, in Davenant's *The Siege of Rhodes*. Alphonso stands for Christian honour, his couplets warming to the challenge of defeating the Muslim enemy ('My Sword against proud *Solyman* I draw, / His cursed Prophet, and his sensual law')[41]. In his second scene, his report of the first skirmish is given in the form of a song in six quatrains – a sign that Davenant recruited him with his singing voice in mind. For all his romantic heroics, the plot leaves him upstaged by Betterton's Solyman, a role with approximately twice the number of lines. Alphonso's bride, Ianthe, is captured by Solyman's army but released on the Sultan's orders so that she and Alphonso can return to Sicily. Initially Alphonso concedes that Solyman is, after all, a 'wondrous enemy' and a 'Christian Turk'.[42] Then jealousy takes over and he resolves to confront Solyman in battle.

---

[39] See later, p. 25. The original is kept at Magdalen College Oxford; copies are in the British Museum's Burney Collection of Theatrical Portraits, vol.4 no.140, p. 85. A portrait advertised by the Philip Mould gallery in 2024 as being of Harris is in fact of Joseph Harris of the King's Company.

[40] Anthony Aston, *A Brief Supplement to Colley Cibber Esq. His Lives of the Famous Actors and Actresses* (London, 1747).

[41] Sir William Davenant, *The Siege of Rhodes* (London: Henry Herringman, 1663), p. 6.

[42] Davenant, *The Siege of Rhodes*, pp. 21–2.

Wounded, he departs asking to 'mourn away [his] sin'.[43] The play was popular, running well into July.

Toward the latter end of the run Harris learned a further role in a Davenant revival. Young Palatine in *The Wits*, a play from the 1630s, lives 'on his exhibition' (i.e. scholarship) and is constantly bailed out by his wealthy brother, played by Betterton. The Elder Palatine's imminent arrival is announced in what must have been taken as a nod back to *The Siege of* Rhodes: sarcastically, his younger brother says 'he moves like some / Assyrian Prince'.[44] Harris's role drew on his capacity to play the cynical libertine and con artist, but one whose charms are subject to brotherly put-downs. 'Brother', warns the Elder Palatine, 'I came / To be your wise example in the Arts'. The Younger Palatine gets his own back with a series of pranks and is rewarded with one of his brother's estates. He has proved, after all, the superior wit.

With Horatio and Sir Andrew Aguecheek, apparently dating from 24 August and 11 September 1661 respectively, Harris reverted to roles in which he was Betterton's sidekick. Hamlet proved an extraordinary success for Betterton; he would continue to play the role into his seventies, his performance immortalized by Colley Cibber's recollection of the moment when his Hamlet first set eyes on the Ghost.[45] No account survives of Betterton's Sir Toby Belch, but that corpulent trickster role is devoted partly to humiliating Sir Andrew, butt of coarse jokes and a hopeless suitor who anticipates, with broad comedy, *Othello*'s Roderigo. We might speculate that Harris's trade profile caused some mirth in the company; Sir Andrew laments his failure to follow the arts, bemoaning its impact on his hair.[46]

With Davenant's *Love and Honour*, first noted on 21 October 1661, Harris returned to the conventions of pre-war tragi-comedy. His Prince Prospero is a love rival to his friend Alvaro, played by Betterton. Prospero loses out in the ultimate apportioning of marital partners. Harris also lost out in the apportioning of costumes. John Downes reported that the show included the robes worn at Westminster Abbey that year. In studied observance of their relative distinction, Harris was loaned the Duke of York's coronation suit, and Betterton the King's. Downes went on to write that *Love and Honour* 'Produc'd to the Company great Gain and Estimation from the Town'[47] – a boost to Harris's finances as a shareholder but perhaps not to his ego. Samuel Pepys saw the production three times in a single week without mentioning Harris. Come Massinger's *The Bondman* in

---

[43] Davenant, *The Siege of Rhodes*, p. 45.
[44] Davenant, *The Wits* (London: Bedel and Collins, 1665), p. 7. [45] Cibber, *Apology*, p. 77.
[46] Shakespeare, *Twelfth Night*, I.iii.86–7.
[47] John Downes, *Roscius Anglicanus; or an Historical View of the Stage*, ed. Judith Milhous and Robert D. Hume (London: Society for Theatre Research, 1987), p. 52.

November, a play in which Harris may not have had a role, Betterton had confirmed his place in Pepys's mind as 'the best actor in the world'.[48]

Nevertheless, Harris's next new role established him as the company's first-choice romantic lead. Abraham Cowley's comedy, *Cutter of Coleman Street*, is an updated version of his play *The Guardian* (1642). The first known performance, on 16 December 1661, saw Harris in the role of Truman Junior, a young lover whose girlfriend has failed to gain his father's approval. It is a substantial part abounding in orthodox sentiments of devotion, jealousy, rage, and ultimately penitence. The life of the play is carried by a set of richly drawn comic roles, foremost among them the dispossessed Colonel Jolly, played by Betterton. When Harris was cast as Romeo in March 1662 he may have thought he was at last coming into his own. But if Pepys is to be believed, the production was a disaster: not only did he think the play 'the worst that ever I heard in my life', it was 'the worst acted that ever I saw these people do'. This was the first performance, and it made Pepys resolve never to attend a first performance again (a resolution he failed to keep), because none of the actors could remember their lines properly: 'they were all of them out more or less'.[49] When the prompter John Downes recalled the production, he signally failed to mention a long run, recalling instead a mispronunciation of the word 'count' that brought the house down.[50] It was not uncommon for actors to take a relaxed approach to learning lines when they judged a play unlikely to last. Even so, the most charitable explanation of Harris's particular failure in a title role is that he was struggling to keep pace with the relentless schedule of performances.

The absence of evidence of his involvement in April 1662 revivals of Fletcher and Rowley's *The Maid in the Mill* or Massinger's *The Bondman* cannot be taken as an absence of activity; such is the patchy nature of the records. He probably reprised Alphonso when *The Siege of Rhodes* was revived in May. Soon after, he was in trouble. Davenant had been in a long-running dispute with the Master of the Revels, Sir Henry Herbert, over the latter's claim that licensing fees were due for both new plays and revivals. On 20 June 1662 Herbert sued Davenant for a year's worth of outstanding fees; Davenant countered with a petition that was referred to the Lord High Chancellor and Lord Chamberlain.[51] Meanwhile one of Herbert's deputies, Edward Thomas, appeared at the Duke's Theatre, presumably to demand payment. According to records of the Middlesex magistracy, twelve of the actors, including Harris and Betterton, 'riotously assembled together and

---

[48] Pepys, *Diary*, 4 November 1661 (II.207). No cast lists survive for Restoration productions of the play.
[49] Pepys, *Diary*, 1 March 1662 (III.39). [50] Downes, *Roscius Anglicanus*, p. 53.
[51] *Document Register* nos.142 & 143.

Restoration Acting and Other Business   15

assaulted [him] and beat him and maltreated him, and held him their prisoner for the space of two hours'. Summoned to the bench, all twelve admitted the charge and got off surprisingly lightly with a fine of 3s 4d each.[52] It was the actors, not Davenant, who bore the responsibility. As two of the ten actor-shareholders, Harris and Betterton had particular cause to worry about the addition of unnecessary licensing costs to the theatre, and seemed prepared to use any means to defend their interest. While the incident must have played a role in forcing Davenant to reach terms with Herbert (thus reluctantly following the example his rival manager at the King's Company, Thomas Killigrew), it does not appear to have damaged Harris's standing with the authorities.

Throughout the early 1660s he maintained his premises in the Strand, taking on commissions for seals. As a member of the Clothworkers' Company he faced a 2s fine if he failed to attend a quarter-day meeting.[53] Now, as a Company member and prominent actor who had been recruited by Davenant with painting skills to his name, he was required to take part in an event that combined the scenic, kinetic, and musical excitement of live theatre with the solemnity of civic duty. In August 1662, by way of celebrating the appointment of their own Master, Sir John Robinson, as Lord Mayor, the Clothworkers mounted an entertainment called *London's Triumph*. It was the work of John Tatham, a minor royalist playwright of the pre-war years who turned his hand to five other pageants between 1660 and 1664. The published text recalls 'severall Delightfull Scænes, both upon the Water and Land', and lists an order of proceedings intermingled with semi-dramatic episodes and songs.[54]

London's Triumph began at seven in the morning with a procession from Clothworkers' Hall, near the corner of Fenchurch Street and Mincing Lane. After the Master, the Wardens, and their assistants came 'The Livery', 'in Gowns faced with Budge [i.e. leather], and their Hoods'.[55] Between 300 and 400 others followed, including 36 trumpeters, four of whom were, like Harris, in the service of the Duke of York. Up Gracechurch Street they marched, then Bishopsgate, then the long stretch beside London Wall before turning down to the Guildhall and from there making for 'their severall Barges' at Three Cranes Wharf, where they embarked for Westminster. After a brief ceremony, the party returned down river to Baynard's Castle, near St Paul's. Near the school of that name the new Lord Mayor was 'entertained by the first Scene, representing a piece of Fortification, like the Tower of *London*'. The scene's focus was on the

---

[52] *Document Register* no.144. The sum approximates to between £40 and £50 in current values.
[53] William Herbert, *The History of the Twelve Great Livery Companies of London*, 2 vols. (London: William Herbert, 1836–7), II.657.
[54] John Tatham, *London's Triumph* (London: H. Brown, 1662).
[55] Tatham, *London's Triumph*, p. 1.

business that would occupy the latter part of Harris's career. Here were 'persons Flatting and Coyning of Money', as though labouring at the Royal Mint, then located in premises along the Tower wall.[56]

In rhyming couplets of no great distinction, the Mayor was addressed at length by 'a person mounted and fitted like a Souldier' before moving on to Cheapside, where a further scene showed a Master Clothworker 'under a seeming Oak', arborial symbol of the monarchy.[57] Then came the comic highlight. Enter a man dressed as the Company's icon, the sixteenth-century clothier Jack O'Newbury, riding a ram. Tatham itemized his tall hat, jewelled and feathered, a ruff, a russet-coloured coat, a white satin doublet, and a sword and dagger.[58] Perched on the ram, this extraordinary figure addressed the Mayor, again in halting couplets, before a part song given by 'two old Women' and a chorus of 'the whole body of the Work-folk'. Turning north off Cheapside, the party found a further scene at the end of St Lawrence Lane, this time of a ship and a sea lion with 'a Tryton on the back, playing on Musick'. This symbolic representation of trade, a particular compliment to Sir John Robinson's experience as 'a Merchant trading in several parts of the World', focused on a character identified only as 'an *Asian*'. Of all the speaking roles in the pageant, it is the one that requires the most chameleon-like qualities of its speaker and the most developed contribution from an accomplished actor. We know that professional actors took part in the civic pageants of the early seventeenth century, and there is no reason to assume they did not after the Restoration.[59] It is possible that Betterton himself, fresh from playing Solyman the Magnificent in *The Siege of Rhodes*, took part, but the obligation to be involved lay on Harris as a member of the Clothworkers' Company.

He would go on to carve out his own line in eastern roles: the title role in Roger Boyle, Earl of Orrery's *Mustapha* (1665); Prexaspes in Elkanah Settle's *Cambyses* (1671); Muly Labas in the same author's *The Empress of Morocco* (1673), Zungteus in his *The Conquest of China* (1675) and Ulama in his *Ibrahim the Illustrious Bassa* (1676); and Cassander in Samuel Pordage's *The Siege of Babylon* (1677). To a degree each of those roles embodied the ideology acted

---

[56] Tatham, *London's Triumph*, p. 5.
[57] See, for example, Simon Schama, *Landscape and Memory* (London: Harper Collins, 1995), pp. 135–242.
[58] Tatham, *London's Triumph*, p. 7.
[59] See Tracey Hill, *Pageantry and Power: A Cultural History of the Early Modern Lord Mayor's Show, 1585–1639* (Manchester and New York: Manchester University Press, 2010), pp. 144–6. Even actors as eminent as Edward Alleyn, Richard Burbage and John Lowin took part in civic pageantry. On the relationships between the livery companies and professional actors, see David Kathman, 'Grocers, Goldsmiths and Drapers: Freemen and Apprentices in the Elizabethan Theatre', *Shakespeare Quarterly* 55.1 (2004), 1–49, and Paula R. Backscheider, 'Beyond City Walls: Restoration Actors in the Drapers' Company', *Theatre Survey* 45.1 (May 2004), 75–87.

out by the '*Asian*' in Tatham's pageant, asserting racial and mercantile superiority through the capacity to take possession of the skin and the mannerisms of the ethnic other. In his own Clothworkers' pageant of 1694, Settle would praise the Company and the industries it fostered as key to an 'Imperial Britannia' that was 'so formidable to her foes, and so potent to her friends'.[60]

The 1662–63 theatrical season would prove pivotal in Harris's career, his relations with the Court, and his marriage. September and October 1662 saw him in roles of anguished masculinity: the lycanthropic Ferdinand in Webster's *The Duchess of Malfi* and Beauprés in Thomas Porter's highly popular *The Villain*, where Harris's character is tricked into murdering his own wife. Porter's irregular blank verse is punctuated by passages of rhyming couplets – a reminder of the many speech and singing styles Harris was required to master so early in his acting career. Come the turn of the year, a further new role positioned him amid ideological controversy that would haunt the rest of his acting and other careers.

Samuel Tuke's play, *The Adventures of Five Hours*, was a runaway success in January 1663. Downes remembered performances for '13 Days together, no other Play intervening', while Pepys rhapsodized about its plot, which John Evelyn found 'incomparable'.[61] Harris played Don Antonio, an honourable aristocrat in love, his language as 'stiffe and formal' as Evelyn had declared it and with sentiments that sat uneasily with Harris's hustling life ('I have been taught . . . to Deserve, / But not to Seek Reward').[62] Far more than any other play in which Harris had appeared, *The Adventures* paid tribute to the Catholic patronage of the Duke's Company – a counterblast, perhaps, to the pungent anti-Catholicism of *The Duchess of Malfi*. A love and honour comedy set in Seville, it was the work of a man prominent among Catholics loyal to the King. When Charles's mother, Henrietta Maria, objected to the Duke of York's marriage to Anne Hyde, the Earl of Clarendon's daughter, Samuel Tuke was sent to the French court to appease her; on the death of Cardinal Mazarin in 1661, he was sent again as Charles II's representative.[63] And when Harris stepped out to play Don Antonio, he was performing a version of one of England's leading Catholic noblemen. Tuke dedicated his play to Henry Howard, later the 6th Duke of Norfolk, praising his typically 'Steady Virtue' and proclaiming him the model for the character of Antonio. This was the first of many occasions during the

---

[60] Elkanah Settle, 'To the Honourable Company of Clothworkers', in *The Triumphs of London Prepared for the Entertainment of the Right Honourable Sir Thomas Lane* (London: Richard Baldwin, 1694), pp. 1–2.
[61] Downes, *Roscius Anglicanus*, p. 54. Pepys, *Diary,* 8 January 1663 (IV.8); Evelyn, *The Diary of John Evelyn*, ed. E. S. De Beer (Oxford: Oxford University Press, 1959), 8 January 1663.
[62] Samuel Tuke, *The Adventures of Five Hours* (London: Henry Herringman, 1663), p. 17.
[63] 'Sir Samuel Tuke', DNB XIX.1227.

1660s when Harris became known either for sympathetic portrayals of Catholic figures or for making fun of their opponents. It may also have been the moment when he began to sense that he had an influential group of supporters who could be trusted to back him in his hour of need.

For his next new role, a rival figure of influence floated into view. Robert Stapylton's *The Slighted Maid*, first noted in February 1663, was the work of a former Benedictine monk who had converted to Protestantism. It is dedicated to Charles II's illegitimate son, James, Duke of Monmouth, symbolic leader of the opposition to the Duke of York's accession. When Pepys saw the play he was too distracted by an actress's 'very fine legs' to pay much attention to Harris's Salerno, but the congruence of man and role would linger in his mind when he learned, that summer, of the dispute that saw Harris take a stand against Davenant. Salerno is described in the *dramatis personae* as 'An aery young Prince, who (being refused by his Love) is a pretender unto Mistresses'.[64]

In July 1663, Samuel Pepys heard from a shoemaker called Wotton that Harris had gone on strike:

> [Harris] grew very proud and demanded 20 *l* for himself extraordinary there, [more] than Batterton or anybody else, upon every new play, and 10 *l* upon every Revive – which, with other things, Sir W Davenant would not give him; and so he swore he would never act there more – in expectation of being received in the other House; but the King will not suffer it, upon Sir W Davenant's desire that he would not; for then he might shut up house, and that is true. He tells me that his going is at present a great loss to the house. And that he fears he has a stipend from the other House privately.[65]

It is a vivid picture of a man who knew his value to the company and sought to exploit it by fair means or foul. Recruited as an outsider on terms 'equal with the highest', he nevertheless hustled to out-earn his colleagues, willing to undertake any subterfuge to get his way. Should we take it as a sign of Harris's 'celebrity' that Pepys learned about the episode from someone in such a humble walk of life? Not necessarily. Wotton's Fleet Street premises were a five-minute walk from the Lincoln's Inn Fields playhouse on Portugal Row. The shoemaker was one tradesman passing on neighbourhood gossip about another.

Harris's strike action had a domestic context in the financial crisis that was starting to derail his marriage. During his period of absence from the Duke's Company, he travelled to Bath, leaving his wife Anne with a document that gave her power of attorney in his absence. He wrote to her for money, so she borrowed from a woman called Mary Ingoldsby, who appears to have been a

---

[64] Pepys, *Diary*, 23 February 1663 (IV.56); Robert Stapylton, *The Slighted Maid* (London: Thomas Dring, 1663), np.
[65] Pepys, *Diary*, 22 July 1663 (IV.239).

pawnbroker. The lease of the Strand premises stood as security against the loan.[66] Anne would go back to Ingoldsby for items her husband required for a party, and the list demonstrates Harris's growing fondness for the high life: silver tankards, 'porringers' (i.e. shallow bowls) and silver spoons, a watch with forty diamonds, pearl necklaces, eight gold, ruby, emerald, and diamond rings, and a satin petticoat richly laced with silver. Once the party was over, and anxious to raise some money herself, Anne took some of the items not to Ingoldsby but to a different pawnbroker. When Harris found out, he recovered the goods but failed to return them to Ingoldsby. Then he burned the power of attorney lest it should incriminate him. Mary Ingoldsby would continue to haunt the Harrises at least until 1670.[67] Henry's actions, in particular his failure to appear in Chancery, resulted in an order to settle with Ingoldsby and a brief arrest for contempt of court.[68]

However, as a liveried servant of the Duke of York, he knew he could enjoy a degree of protection. In April 1670 two men named Hide and Gosse would make the mistake of arresting him for debt without permission from the Lord Chamberlain. It was they who were arrested.[69] So, when Harris went on strike in 1663, it seems likely that he felt he had already built up sufficient credit to defy an explicit ban on actors changing companies. Remarkably, his plan worked. Still more remarkably, he managed to acquire a court position along the way.

Less than a month into his protest, on 6 August 1663, Harris was appointed to the role of Yeoman of the Revels.[70] The title had existed since 1534, when John Farlyon was appointed to it, and the job description had not changed significantly when Harris received his grant. He was to be 'Keeper of our [i.e. the Court's] Vestures or Apparell of a[ll and] singular our Masques Revells and disguisings'. Maintaining costumes and props came with a further obligation to oversee 'the Apparell a[nd] Trappers of all and singular our horses ordained and appointed and hereafter [to] be ordained and appointed for our Iusts and Turneys'.[71] By the seventeenth century jousts and tournaments were, of course, theatrical rather than martial. An extensive literature translated from European languages suggests a nascent and nostalgic medievalism that chimed with

---

[66] Details of Anne's dealings with Mary Ingoldsby are in Arches E6/138.
[67] Mary Ingoldsby began her suit with an approach to the Lord Chamberlain on December 15, 1668 (*Document Register* no. 457), clearing the way for proceedings in the Court of Chancery to begin with her bill of complaint dated 16 March 1669. The proceedings continued into 1670 (National Archives, C10/110/54 and C6/195/60).
[68] Arches E6/138. On 15 December 1668 Harris was ordered by Lord Chamberlain Manchester to settle with Ingoldsby or be sued (*Document Register* no.465).
[69] *Document Register* no.553.   [70] *Document Register* no.233.
[71] Grant of office by Charles II to Henry Harris, reproduced in J. O. Halliwell-Phillipps, *A Collection of Ancient Documents Respecting the Office of the Master of the Revels* (London: T. Richards, 1870), p. 62.

Harris's own experience of playing characters from history.[72] He may already have been experienced in equine business: his wife Anne would later attest that in the early years of their marriage he often travelled to Europe, buying selling horses and velvet saddles across the Channel. If acquiring 'trappers' (i.e. cloth, leather or metal coverings for the royal horses) came naturally, Harris's travels were prompted by local scarcity. England's leather industry was barely keeping pace with population growth, while material of the right quality for royal use was more likely to be found in Holland or Spain; an on-going trade war with France made French goods less attractive.[73]

Harris's grant of office as Yeoman specified a limited number terms and conditions. He was to enjoy the role for life, regardless of the royal succession, and to maintain a deputy or deputies. His basic allowance would be sixpence a day, payable annually in arrears. He would also be allowed a new livery coat each year 'such as the Yeomen Officers of our Household have', and have the use of 'one Sufficient house or Mancion' for 'the sure better and safe keeping' of all 'Vestures, Apparell and Trappers'.[74] The grant's concluding words offer the reassurance that he would enjoy the same terms as his predecessors, but it withholds 'Expresse mencion of the true yearely value' of any further benefits or gifts. Since the Yeoman was expected to buy any new 'Vestures, Apparell and Trappers' and then claim the money back via the slow lane that was the Lord Chamberlain's office, any holder of the office exposed himself to significant financial risk. During the reign of Elizabeth I, it was said that no one could undertake the role on the basis of the salary alone without being 'muche hindered and in danger of undoynge unless he be of greate wealthe'.[75]

If that were not enough to warn Harris of the risks, he had a fine example of hindering and undoing in the shape of his immediate predecessor. John Carey (or Carew) had been Yeoman of the Revels since 25 June 1660.[76] Carey's responsibilities had exceeded the usual job description; they included fitting out the Cockpit Theatre in Whitehall. A succession of bills for the period 1661–2 cites his acquisition of chairs, tables, candlesticks, a mirror, a stage bed with 'red Tafatty coverlett', and more than a hundred yards of green baize for the stage and seating areas.[77] Like other officers of the Carolean Court, he

---

[72] Among many examples, André Favin, *The Theatre of Honour and Knighthood* (London: William Jaggard, 1623); William Segar, *Honour Military and Civill Contained in Four Books* (London: Robert Barker, 1602); and John Selden, *The Duello or Single Combat from Antiquity* (London: John Helme, 1610).
[73] See Leslie A. Clarkson, 'The English Leather Industry in the Sixteenth and Seventeenth Centuries, (1563–1700)'. Unpublished PhD thesis, University of Nottingham, 1960.
[74] Halliwell-Phillipps, *A Collection of Ancient Documents*, p. 63.
[75] Halliwell-Phillipps, *A Collection of Ancient Documents*, p. 71.
[76] www.british-history.ac.uk/office-holders/vol11/pp114-115
[77] *Document Register* nos.89, 161, 178.

sometimes had to wait months for reimbursement; even his salary might not materialize. Only three months before he surrendered the role to Harris, Carey petitioned Lord Chamberlain Manchester to complain that neither his salary, board and rental allowances, nor daily stipend had been paid. For his salary he gave a figure of £50. That was rounded up from £46 11s 8d, in other words the salary that was paid over and above the sixpenny daily fee. It was, he argued, not enough to live on.[78] Manchester was sympathetic but wanted to probe details of the allowances. A subsequent report specified the sums involved: in addition to his salary, Carey was owed £13 6s 8d for board, a £15 per annum housing allowance, and a stipend of 6d per day which Manchester recommended should be doubled (the recommendation was accepted).[79] So Carey's total pay was approximately £90 a year, or something like £22,500 in current values – sufficient justification for his claim that he could not live on his Yeoman's pay alone. A Yeoman of the Revels needed other sources of income. In Carey's case, one other is known, and it too has a theatrical connection. He owned land described as a 'garden' adjoining the site of the Lincoln's Inn Fields theatre. In January 1661 Sir William Davenant bought a twenty-year lease from him for a four-foot-wide strip needed for the theatre's auxiliary accommodation.[80] He was familiar enough with Davenant to witness, in December 1662, an agreement to buy off the theatrical entrepreneur George Jolly.[81]

How did Harris come to be appointed in Carey's place? It is safe to assume from the land deal and the Duke's Company's occasional performances at Court that the two men at least knew of each other. It would not be surprising if Harris heard of Carey's complaints about his salary and saw an opportunity, however precarious, at a time when his own position in the Duke's Company was on the line. Selling offices remained a common practice, with a year's salary about par for the fee. The declaration of Harris's appointment describes Carey as having 'voluntarily resigned'. Carey was probably dissatisfied with his meagre pay rise and fed up with paying out for goods with no certainty of prompt reimbursement. A fortnight after he relinquished the role, he was paid the considerable sum of £173 (around £43,000 in current values, and almost twice his annual earnings from the role) for costs incurred as far back as June 1660.[82] What had looked in 1660 like a tidy sinecure had turned into a financial drain, making Carey another victim of the culture of excessive promising and under-delivering that characterized the financial establishment of Charles II's Court. Still, the

---

[78] *Document Register* no.207.   [79] *Document Register* nos.215 & 218.
[80] *Document Register* no.57.   [81] *Document Register* no.179.
[82] *Document Register* no.239. The document specifies payments to three servants who waited on the actors, and for silk curtains.

Yeoman role was hardly full-time and in theory a comfortable one if it could be made to work alongside other commitments.

Tempting though it is to conclude that Harris's appointment was part of the deal that saw him return in October 1663 to the Duke's Company, and that Carey was leaned on from above to make way, the gap of two months between the appointment and Harris's reinstatement as an actor suggests that the two events were not connected in quite that way. More plausible is the idea that an actor withholding services needed to find an insurance policy. To secure it, he needed friends in high places.

Carey had done the hard yards of fitting out the Cockpit Theatre, but the bigger task was yet to come: the fitting out of the Hall Theatre at Whitehall. Fortunately for Harris, responsibility for the work fell to the architect John Webb (Harris's first known activity concerning the space was to act in it by taking the title role in Orrery's *Mustapha*).[83] But there were numerous attempts to reshape the Hall Theatre during the next decade, for which Harris bore the responsibility of ordering materials. Under him worked a small team, most prominently the 'Theatre-Keeper', a role undertaken by two generations of Johnson men, George and Philip, until 1677, when John Clarke took over, continuing almost to the end of Harris's period as Yeoman.[84] Early in his tenure, Harris had been required to surrender one of the perks enjoyed by Carey. The 'Lodgings in the Cockpitt that Mr Harris yeoman of the revels now possesseth' were, as of May 1664, to be occupied by George Johnson – a sure sign that Johnson was a more regular presence than the Yeoman.

Complementing Harris's life in the theatre, the new role could be fitted around his acting commitments. It gave him extra status in the company and, since his new terms were equal to Betterton's, probably meant that his total earnings overtook those of his co-star, who himself was reported by Pepys to have become 'rich' as early as 1662.[85] Harris certainly showed little indication of wanting to surrender the Yeomanship, as Carey had. In fact he held the office for the rest of his life, surviving the regime changes of 1685 (James II) and William III (1688), as his grant of office had specified. There was no urgency to replace him either in life or death. His successor, Thomas Warters, was not appointed until January 1706, nearly two years after Harris died.

Harris was offered terms identical to Carey's, including the uplift agreed by Lord Chamberlain Manchester. Judith Milhous has calculated that his 10 per cent shareholding in the Duke's Company was worth approximately £66 per annum, on top of the salary he drew as an actor. Rent from subletting and the

---

[83] Eleanore Boswell, *The Restoration Court Stage* (Cambridge, MA: Harvard University Press, 1932), p. 28. *Mustapha* was performed there on 3 June 1665.
[84] Boswell, *The Restoration Court Stage*, p. 277.   [85] Pepys, *Diary*, 22 October 1662; III.233.

Yeomanship meant he would now have four sources of income. That did not prevent him, four years into the Yeomanship, from petitioning for a pay rise.[86] Whether he received the additional 6d a day he requested is not known. He certainly had an increasing number of creditors at his door – on his wife's account, he would claim.

Previous Yeomen of the Revels had also been performers. Richard Gibson, who held the role in the early sixteenth century, was an 'interluder', while John Holt, from the early Elizabethan years, was a 'mummer' with a sideline in coaching boys from Westminster School.[87] Harris was perhaps unique in marshalling the diplomatic skills needed to cope with a succession of Masters in the Revels Office. His first was Sir Henry Herbert, whose servant he had been complicit in beating in 1662 (another indication, possibly, that his appointment as Yeoman was settled several grades above Herbert's). Thomas Killigrew, who took office following Herbert's death in 1673, was manager of the rival King's Company, and had probably been party to Harris's attempted defection in the summer of 1663. Killigrew's successor was his son Charles, who took office in 1677 following a bitter legal dispute and remained in post until 1725. Charles Killigrew is one of the principal antagonists of Cibber's *Apology*, where he stands condemned for caring little about the theatre and for demonstrating a 'zealous severity' in censoring plays. Zeal, at least, is a quality hard to reconcile with what is known of Henry Harris, yet the two men would survive the regime changes of 1685 and 1688.[88]

When Harris returned to the Duke's Company, puffed up by court preferment, Pepys again got wind of the news from his shoemaker. '[B]y the Duke of Yorkes persuasion', he wrote, 'Harris is come again to Sir W Davenant upon his terms that he demanded'. The backstairs lobbying is worth spelling out: even though the King had supported Davenant's position, he was persuaded by his brother the Duke that Harris was too great an asset to the company to be denied. Pepys predicted the effect on Harris's ego: the outcome would 'make him very high and proud'. Part of the blame, Pepys reflected, lay with the King and the general adulation of Harris had attracted. Shoemaker Wotton had initially reported 'that the fellow grew very proud of late, the King and everybody else crying him up so high, and that above Baterton, he being a more ayery man, as he is endeed'. *Ayery* – the quality that had made him an obvious choice for Salerno in Stapylton's *The Slighted Maid*.[89] In 1663 it might mean speculative, imaginative, merry, and sprightly; or, less flatteringly, flimsy and superficial. None of those were qualities people associated with the studiously professional Thomas

---

[86] *Document Register* no.410.
[87] E. K. Chambers, *The Elizabethan Stage*, 4 vols (Oxford: Clarendon Press, 1923), II.319 & 324.
[88] Cibber, *Apology*, p. 184.   [89] See earlier, p. 18.

Betterton, and it was to him Pepys's thoughts turned when he added a waspish tail sting to his report of Harris's actions. For all Harris's popularity among playgoers royal and otherwise, 'they all say [Betterton] doth act some parts that none but himself can do'.[90] The record of Harris's supporting performances in the later 1660s suggests that for all his 'ayery' pride, Harris knew it.

Analysis of his roles in the season of his return suggests he did not take full financial advantage of his new deal. Evidence exists of only three new roles between October 1663 and July 1664, none of them particularly demanding. But that statistic is, of course, consistent with a wish to extract as much money from acting as he could while moderating his commitments in a way that allowed him to pursue other work. His new roles up to the end of 1664 often seem to reflect on his desertion in the summer of 1663, and on the contrast between his private character and that of Betterton.

When Davenant decided to stage Shakespeare and Fletcher's *Henry VIII* – a play Pepys described as 'rare' – it was to be offered as a Christmas and New Year spectacular, 'all new clothed in proper habits' and with 'new scenes'.[91] One of those 'proper habits', a cardinal's cape and hat, was worn by Harris in the role of Wolsey, his success illustrated literally and symbolically by the Greenhill portrait. Like Mercutio in *Romeo and Juliet*, Wolsey allows an actor to make a scintillating impression before disappearing at the end of the third act for whatever alternative pursuits he seeks. In the winter of 1663/4, the role bristled with allusions to Harris's treachery. Notoriously greedy, the trusted first minister turns out to have been in secret correspondence with the Pope. In the showdown scene, III.ii, Betterton's Henry laid down the law: 'say withal / Whether you are bound to us, or no'. Responding with twisted humility, Harris's Wolsey swore his allegiance, 'Which ever has and ever shall be growing'. In his farewell speech, he acknowledges the absolute power of royal favour. Without it, 'he falls like Lucifer, / Never to hope again'.[92] At the first performance, the King and the Duke of York were there to enjoy the irony.[93]

John Downes contextualized Harris's performance by focusing largely on Betterton, who had been 'instructed in [his role] by Sir William, who had it from old Mr Lowin that had his instructions from Mr Shakespeare himself'. There is a shade of two-edged praise in Downes's subsequent assertion that 'Mr Harris's performance of Cardinal Wolsey was little inferior' to Betterton's of Henry. There was no direct line connecting him to Shakespeare, but he did with 'such just state, port and mien that I dare affirm, none has hitherto equalled it'.[94] In

---

[90] Pepys, *Diary*, 24 October 1663.
[91] Pepys, *Diary*, 22 December 1663; on costumes, Downes, *Roscius Anglicanus*, pp. 55–56.
[92] *King Henry VIII*, III.ii.169–372.   [93] Pepys, *Diary*, 22 December 1663.
[94] Downes, *Roscius Anglicanus*, pp. 55–56.

drawing that distinction, Downes was highlighting two approaches to acting. Betterton reproduced instructions to create a performance that was 'right and just', the outcome of sustained immersion in the past. Harris, by contrast, was a charismatic presence, an embodiment of natural rather than learned grace – a possessor, perhaps, of that elusive commodity, charisma, yet caring less than he once had about leading roles.

Two paintings emphasize the contrast. Where Betterton owned a painting of Henry VIII thought to be by Holbein, Harris had himself painted as Wolsey (see Fig.1).[95] Joseph Roach writes of the 'role-icon', a type of part that clings to actors and perpetuates them in the memory of audiences.[96] Betterton's, in Roach's view, was that of the 'tragedy king', a view complicated by Judith Milhous's prior inventory of Betterton's roles, where men-about-town feature far more frequently than the twenty or so kings in his repertory.[97] To the extent that Harris was (or had) a 'role-icon', our best guess is the type in which Greenhill painted him, but his total of four Cardinals was far outnumbered by courtiers and assorted other gentlemen. Perhaps the very idea of the 'role-icon', drawn as it is from schematic Hollywood casting processes, is too restrictive for the rapid turnover of seventeenth-century theatre. In Betterton's case it re-clothes a conventional wisdom about his career that

Figure 1 Henry Harris as Cardinal Wolsey, engraved from a portrait by John Greenhill.

---

[95] For Betterton's painting of Henry VIII, see Hooke, *Pinacotheca Bettertonaeana*, no.19.
[96] Roach, *It*, p. 40.
[97] Judith Milhous, 'An Annotated Census of Thomas Betterton's Roles, 1659-1710', *Theatre Notebook* 29 (1975), 33–45 (part 1) and 85–94 (part 2).

Milhous had already exploded. In Harris's, it seems rash to assume that one picture makes an icon.

Although *Henry VIII* was a considerable commercial success (Downes mentions a run of '15 days together'), it left Pepys cold. '[M]ade up of a great many patches' was his verdict on the play. His sole pleasure was in the 'shows and processions' reminiscent of the street pageantry in which Harris had participated the year before.[98] Bumper profits helped reconcile Harris to the Duke's Company, but in a particular way. While there is no indication of further disputes, repertory evidence suggests that Davenant continued to find ways of exploiting the earlier quarrel as well as the personal contrasts between Harris and Betterton. March 1664 saw the premiere of George Etherege's first play, *The Comical Revenge*. Harris played Sir Frederick Frollick, a blundering, gambling drunk and cousin to Betterton's solemnly honourable Lord Beaufort. 'What, my lord', exclaims Frederick to Beaufort, 'as studious as a country vicar on a Saturday in the afternoon?' Beaufort has the last word: it is not a sermon but action that he is contemplating, 'wherein there's honour to be gained; and you, cousin, are come luckily to share it'.[99] To be a leading actor and shareholder in a licensed company was, when all was said, a slice of good fortune denied to most members of the profession.

In September 1664 Davenant mounted another Shakespeare and Fletcher play in the form of *The Rivals*, his own adaptation of *The Two Noble Kinsman*. A happy ending was engineered by Betterton's Philander transferring his affections away from the woman also loved by Harris's Theocles. The two men shook hands on it: 'My quarrel here with Theocles shall end,' says Philander. 'I lose a rival and preserve a friend.'[100] Philander's final choice of bride, Celania, was played by Pepys's former maid, Winifred Gosnell. In Celania's duet with Theocles, she sang out of tune. Harris came to the rescue by following her – the act not only of an accomplished musician but of a man who had learned, after all, to be a decent trouper.[101] Rewarded with the title role and a second opportunity to wear the Duke of York's robes in the Earl of Orrery's *Henry the Fifth* in August 1664, Harris was becoming a firm favourite of Pepys, who admired him 'more than ever' for his performance in a lost play unpromisingly called *Worse and Worse*.[102]

A further leading role in an Orrery play, *Mustapha* (April 1665), as well as a Macduff (an enhanced role in Davenant's version of *Macbeth*, November

---

[98] Pepys, *Diary*, 1 January 1664.   [99] Etherege, *The Comical Revenge* (London, 1664), p. 49.
[100] *The Rivals*, in *The Works of Sir William Davenant* (London, 1673), p. 117.
[101] Pepys, *Diary*, 10 December 1664.
[102] Pepys, *Diary*, 20 July 1664. The play was an adaptation by George Digby, 2nd Earl of Bristol, probably of Calderón's *Peor está que estaba*.

1664), cemented his reputation as a leader in the company, and at the very time the demands of his second job were increasing. As Yeoman of the Revels he was required to co-ordinate costumes and properties for a court masque in February 1665; in March, he was called on to advise on the condition of the court theatre.[103] But having two jobs and four income streams was still not enough.

4 Petitioning for Seals

Harris had already turned his craft training to account, but come the summer of 1665 and the onset of plague, the need rapidly became more urgent. The public theatres were closed between 5 June 1665 and November the following year, leaving the actors to fall back on whatever other resources they could summon. In 1665 Harris petitioned for another role. He wrote that he had 'been employed by Lord Arlington in engraving several seals for his Majesty's service', hoping they had 'given satisfaction'.[104] Creating the design on paper, applying it to wax, then carving the images in reverse via the wax and after that onto metal for impressing on official documents, with sufficient intricacy to deter forgers, robustness to withstand repeated use, and diplomacy to create an instantly recognizable and suitably flattering portrait of the monarch – engraving seals of state was a highly skilled and responsible occupation that made the practitioner an instrument of state authority and propaganda that reached far beyond the British Isles. Surviving seals used by Charles II show him in impressive detail enthroned and on horseback, the defender of the faith charging into battle. No little skill was involved in executing such work to the satisfaction of so prominent a politician and connoisseur as Sir Henry Bennet, Baron Arlington.

At the time of Harris's 1665 petition, Arlington was Secretary of State for the Southern Department and a key figure in reconciling the wishes of King and Parliament. Experienced in foreign affairs, he spoke more languages than the rest of Charles's cabinet put together. He was also a prominent patron of the arts, using his diplomatic networks to buy or commission paintings and other artefacts for his own and the King's greater glory.[105] His interest in Italian painting and French music suggests a man with a discerning eye who would not lightly have given employment to an actor-cum-engraver, especially when it came to the business of representing the King's person. If Harris's graphic skills were of value to Arlington, so was his prominence in the Duke's Company. When Pepys spotted the actor at a coffee house engaged in 'very witty and pleasant discourse' with 'all the wits of the town', he saw among them another

---

[103] *Document Register* no.311. [104] *CSPD Domestic, Charles II: Addenda*, p. 150.
[105] See Helen Jacobsen, 'Luxury Consumption, Cultural Politics, and the Career of the Earl of Arlington, 1660-1685', *The Historical Journal* 52.2 (June 2009), 295–317.

man of the theatre who had been taken under Arlington's wing.[106] John Dryden, chief playwright of the King's Company, was by marriage within the orbit of James, Duke of York, already believed to be a secret Catholic; Dryden himself would later convert. Suspicions regarding Arlington's own religious inclinations remain unresolved, in spite of strong rumours of a deathbed conversion to Catholicism. A recent essay argues that he was motivated purely by politics, describing him as 'flirting with Catholicism in the hope of improving England's international situation' with the great European powers.[107] As ambassador to Spain in the late 1650s he had become 'obedient to Spanish gold', yet in 1666 he chose a militantly Protestant Dutch wife, Isabella von Nassau.[108] If such political trimming made him a moving target politically (as well as privately wealthy), it also inclined him towards viewing life as a studiously contrived series of masks. It is little wonder that when he was ejected from the Secretaryship of State in 1674, his consolation was to take responsibility for affairs of the stage, as Lord Chamberlain.

Arlington set a powerful example to Harris of manoeuvring in the interests of accumulation. In Harris he found an actor who would himself 'flirt' with varying representations of Catholic clergymen: some tragic, conjuring memories of a lost national past; others merely Machiavellian, stirring hatred of European enemies. The difference between them was that Harris would eventually tire of the juggling act.

Harris showed his characteristic self-assurance in drafting his 1665 petition. What he asked was nothing less than to replace the recently deceased Thomas Simon, an expert senior engraver at the Royal Mint who had probably succumbed to plague. Harris may have been encouraged by the example of the incumbent Chief Engraver, Thomas Rawlins, another thespian-cum-artist; Rawlins's play, *The Rebellion*, had been a topical success before war broke out.[109] Appointed by Charles I in 1645, Rawlins had worked from Oxford while the Protectorate took control of the Mint, then based at the Tower of London. He was reinstated in 1660 but it was the Protectorate's man, Thomas Simon, who was brought in over his head, at a slightly higher salary, to engrave the dies for Charles II's first

---

[106] Pepys, *Diary*, 3 February 1664 (V.37).

[107] Alistair Malcolm, 'Pretending to Be Catholic? Sir Henry Bennet, the Alliance with Spain and Stuart Dalliance with Rome, 1656-62', in Robin Eagles and Coleman A. Dennehy, eds., *Henry Bennet, Earl of Arlington, and his World. Restoration Court, Politics and Diplomacy* (London: Routledge, 2021) pp. 31–51 (43).

[108] On Arlington's Spanish pension, see a report by the Venetian ambassador in Spain, Giacomo Quirini, cited in Jacobsen, 'Luxury Consumption', p. 300.

[109] Thomas Rawlins, *The Rebellion: a Tragedy* (London: Daniel Frere, 1640); the title page describes it as 'acted nine days together and divers times since with good applause, by his Majesties Company of Revells'. This Rawlins is not to be confused with the author of two Duke's Company comedies, *Tom Essence* (first performed 1676) and *Tunbridge-Wells* (first performed 1678).

coinage.[110] However, it soon became clear that Simon's dies (that is, cylindrical pieces of metal used for stamping images onto metal), for all their notable aesthetic refinement, were too fragile for a newly designed mechanical production process, so he was in turn sidelined by the three brothers Roettier, Antwerp engravers who had come to London in 1662. Dining with The Mint's master, Henry Slingsby, Pepys thought their work 'sweeter' but judged Simon's representation of Cromwell to be a better likeness than the Roettiers' of Charles II.[111]

Neither Simon's conspicuous expertise nor the demands of the new production process were a deterrent to the ever-confident Harris. However, even Arlington's protection was not enough to win him the role. His later involvement with The Mint raises doubts about the extent of his skills. It would be five years before a second chance came his way. By then, he would be yet further in Arlington's sphere of influence.

Fortunately for the shareholders of the Duke's Company's theatre, the Great Fire of 1666 did not reach quite so far west as Lincoln's Inn Fields. Nevertheless, governmental caution meant that when the companies were permitted to act again, for two months they did so largely at Court. Harris repeated what by now were stock roles in his repertoire: Antonio in *The Adventures of Five Hours*, Macduff, Sir Frederick in *The Comical Revenge*, and the title roles in Orrery's *Mustapha* and *Henry the Fifth*. During the 1666–67 season he appears to have learned only two new roles: another cardinal in James Shirley's play of that name, and Richmond in John Caryll's *The English Princess*, based on Shakespeare's *Richard III*. Caryll, a noted Catholic apologist, would feature again in one of the Duke's Company's most significant dealings with Arlington.

Harris's relative lack of industry in the 1666–67 season is explained partly by the illness he contracted in February 1667.[112] In addition, supervising the fit-out of the Hall theatre at Court in January 1667 would have been time-consuming, judging by the detailed specification of works that required a substantial team of carpenters, plumbers, plasterers and curtain-hangers, the latter handling '73 yards of fine blue Canvas'.[113] Harris had other worries. Although he had been sworn in as Yeoman of the Revels in August 1663, he still had no written patent guaranteeing him the role for life. A document dated 3 March 1667 orders that the patent be issued, but a month later the process was stopped until further notice.[114] Not until June was the patent issued, and in that month the theatres

---

[110] Challis, *Mint*, p. 350.   [111] Pepys, *Diary*, 9 March 1663 (IV.70).
[112] Pepys, *Diary*, 27 February 1667 (VIII.86), heard that he had recovered.
[113] *Document Register* no.366.
[114] LC 5/138, p. 280 (*Document Register* no.373) and suspension order of 4 April 1667, LC 5/138, p. 369 (*Document Register* no.376).

were closed again when a hostile fleet of Dutch warships threatened an invasion.[115] The period of uncertainty coincided with still greater strains on Harris's private finances and domestic life. On 23 April 1667 he was summoned to appear before the Lord Chamberlain to explain a debt owed to William Watkins, a seller of Indian gowns at the sign of the Peacock in The Strand, and therefore a neighbour of the Harrises.[116] The debt was one of many incurred by Anne, for which Henry, as her husband, was liable. According to a note drawn up by Arlington's secretary on 10 June 1667, Harris was himself owed a large sum of money by the goldsmith Christopher Birkhead, who was under suspicion of having known about an alleged plot to start the Great Fire.[117]

Harris's difficulties were partly addressed by the success, in August 1667, of Dryden's comedy, *Feign'd Innocence*, which John Downes said 'got the Company more Money than any preceding Comedy' apart from Etherege's *The Comical Revenge*.[118] Pepys saw it three times and found it so funny that he had a headache 'all the evening and night with the laughing'.[119] The main attraction was James Nokes as the clownishly inept Sir Martin. Harris played his fixer-cum-manservant Warner, a straight-man part that demanded considerable focus in managing quick-fire dialogue, not to mention restraint in giving space to Nokes's highly expressive facial acting.[120] The knife-edge thrill of playing farce may have led him to view other repertoire less seriously. When the first run of Dryden's play gave way to a revival of Orrery's *Mustapha*, Pepys complained that Harris and Betterton kept corpsing.[121] However unprofessional, it was at least a sign that Harris had settled into a state of *bonhomie* with his fellow lead.

In October 1667 Betterton fell ill and did not act for eight months. Given Harris's behaviour in the summer of 1663, he might have been expected to prove himself in at least some of Betterton's major roles. But a junior actor, John Young, stood in as Macbeth, while William Smith covered Maligni in Porter's *The Villain*.[122] When the company produced the commercially successful adaptation of *The Tempest*, Harris limited himself to playing Ferdinand rather than taking up Prospero's staff.[123] The most likely explanation is that other commitments limited his ability to learn new roles, and that the earlier sense of rivalry with Betterton had vanished. Meanwhile, creditors were circling again.

---

[115] PRO C66/3090, no.13 (*Document Register* no.387); LS1, p. 109.
[116] LC 5/186, fol.137 (*Document Register* no.379).   [117] *CSPD 1667*, p. 168.
[118] Downes, *Roscius Anglicanus*, p. 63.   [119] Pepys, *Diary*, 16 August 1667 (VIII.387).
[120] For Nokes's performance, see Cibber, *Apology*, p. 104. Cibber saw Nokes long after Harris had quit acting but remembered the highlight of his performance as the rapid-fire exchange between Sir Martin and Warner at the end of Act 2.
[121] Pepys, *Diary*, 4 September 1667 (VIII.421).
[122] Pepys, *Diary*, 16 & 24 October 1667 (VIII.482 & 499).
[123] The evidence for Harris's possession of the role is in Pepys, *Diary*, 11 May 1668 (IX.195).

Claims were lodged against him by five different tradesmen between October 1667 and May 1668. On 26 November 1667 Harris was ordered to respond to a man called Thomas Halfpenny. His failure to do so is recognized in an order of 30 November stipulating Halfpenny's right to 'take his free course at Law' should Harris not respond within a fortnight.[124] The pattern was repeated with claims by Robert Bird (January 1668), Richard Snow (February 1668), and a Mr Levett, landlord of the Blue Balls Inn – an unsavoury establishment to which Harris would introduce Pepys.[125] Little wonder that in the midst of those embarrassments Harris petitioned the Treasury for his additional 6d per day as Yeoman of the Revels.[126] The refashioning of the Hall theatre continued to draw on his time, with additional works and deliveries scheduled during February 1668. He was fast discovering for himself what John Carew's example had made clear: that the Yeoman's role suited the already rich.[127] For reasons that are not clear, but seem likely to concern further debts, Harris was even threatened in March 1668 with a legal action by his boss at the Revels Office, Sir Henry Herbert.[128]

With pressures mounting, at the opening of Etherege's second play, *She Would If She Could*, he was thoroughly distracted. Pepys overheard the playwright complaining that the actors 'were out of humour, and had not their parts perfect', and that Harris in particular 'did do nothing, nor could so much as sing a ketch in it'.[129] It was a character role, Sir Joslin, a country knight partial to song, drink and fondling. 'A catch and a glass, / A fiddle and a lass, / What more would an honest man have?' he sang, to Etherege's displeasure.[130] He was redeemed in Pepys's eyes, at least, by singing the epilogue to Davenant's *The Man's the Master* in the style of a street ballad-singer.[131] The play's title was a premonition of what was to come the following week. When Sir William Davenant died at the beginning of April 1668 it was not immediately clear who would take over management of the Duke's Company. His widow Mary maintained a strong interest. The natural heir, Thomas Betterton, was both a superior actor and known to be careful with money. But he was also still recovering from the illness that had kept him from acting since October the previous year. With his Court connections and experience of team leadership

---

[124] For Capell's suit, *Document Register* no.400; for Halfpenny's, *Document Register* nos.404 & 405.
[125] *Document Register* nos.414, 418, 423, 430, 438, 446.
[126] *Document Register* no.410. The petition is dated 17 December 1667.
[127] *Document Register* nos.419, 420, 422, 424.   [128] *Document Register* no.437.
[129] Pepys, *Diary*, 6 February 1668 (IX.54).
[130] In *The Plays of Sir George Etherege*, ed. Michael Cordner (Cambridge: Cambridge University Press, 1982), V.i.527-9 (p. 204).
[131] Pepys, *Diary*, 26 April 1668 (IX.175).

there, as well as his profile as an actor, Harris could also stake a claim. So Lady Mary appointed them both. Doing so, she provided Harris with yet another source of income at a time when he desperately needed it.

His needs, and his ways of managing them, are evident in the friendship he enjoyed with Pepys, which had begun in earnest in 1667. The two men were connected by patronage: Pepys, the official who looked up to the Duke of York as Head of the Navy; Harris, leading member of the Duke's theatre company. Between seven and eight in the evening on 24 January 1667, three people turned up at Pepys's house to join his after-work party. There was Elizabeth Pierce, wife of the Duke of York's surgeon, and 'one dressed like a country-maid, with a straw hatt on', who turned out to be the King's Company actress Elizabeth Knepp, still in costume from an afternoon performance; and there was Henry Harris. Pepys took him aside to show off his study and found him 'a very curious and understanding person in all, pictures and other things – and a man of fine conversation'. When they re-joined the company there was dancing and singing to the music of 'four fiddlers that play very well'. Pepys was struck by Harris's 'Irish song, the strangest in itself and the prettiest sung by him that ever I heard'. After supper, the singing and dancing went on until three in the morning. Knepp started to feel queasy so Elizabeth Pepys found her a bed. Harris had been similarly provided for but insisted on walking home through the drizzling wind. Pepys reflected on an evening 'of the merriest enjoyments', regretting only the 30s he had paid for the fiddlers. Elizabeth Knepp, by contrast, had a price to pay for her attendance. Supposedly checking to see if she was all right, her host woke her. Then he fondled her breasts and kissed them before singing a lullaby.[132]

On 6 January 1668 Pepys blamed his wife for suggesting that Pierce the surgeon and Harris come for lunch. Food was rapidly prepared and again Pepys was struck by the quality of Harris's conversation. This 'excellent person' was 'better qualified for converse' than anyone Pepys knew, 'whether in things of his own trade or of other kinds'. Evidently Harris's adaptability served him well at the dinner table as well as in keeping his head above financial waters. Here was 'a man of great understanding and observation' whose presence was that of a complete gentleman, 'very agreeable in the manner of his discourse'. When Pepys added that he was 'civil as far as is possible' he did not mean *for an actor*, but that he could not imagine anyone more polite.[133]

However, the cost of treating a man mired in debt was mounting. After lunch, Pepys hired a coach to take Harris to the Duke's Theatre, where the actor was due to perform in *The Tempest*. With no room in the pit or galleries, Pepys parted with

---

[132] Pepys, *Diary*, 24 January 1667 (VIII.28-9).   [133] Pepys, *Diary*, 6 January 1668 (IX.13).

20s for box tickets and some oranges. After the show, once Harris had changed, another coach took him back to Pepys's house for supper, song, and dance. After midnight there was sherry and 'an excellent Cake' costing a further 20s until, at two in the morning, Harris departed in yet another coach. The diary entry records that he left with Elizabeth Knepp, the actress apparently sharing the attentions of both navy clerk and actor. After shelling out £3 for the privilege of being entertained by four musicians in the service of the Duke of Buckingham ('the best in Towne'), Pepys consoled himself: he may as well enjoy himself while he was 'able to pay for it or have health to take pleasure in it'.[134]

His next opportunity to indulge that thought came on Sunday, 29 March 1668. Harris came to lunch with John Banister, the King's principal violinist. They were 'most extraordinary company both': Banister 'for music of all sorts', and Harris 'for everything'. Pepys and Harris sang to Banister's theorbo accompaniment, followed by 'very good discourse about music'. Then Harris noticed a portrait of Elizabeth Pepys by John Hales. So complimentary was he that Pepys offered to have Hales paint Harris. In return, Harris dangled a prize Pepys could not resist. Whether through court, trade or coffee house connections, Harris knew the celebrated miniaturist, Samuel Cooper, who had painted the King himself as well as Cromwell and Arlington. If Pepys was agreeable, Harris would have Cooper 'draw' Mrs Pepys. The diary entry suggests it took some persuasion; the fee would, after all, be £30 (around £7,500 in current values).[135] Anxious to cement the relationship, Harris arranged to meet Pepys and Hales the following morning and take them to Cooper's house in Henrietta Street, just off Covent Garden market. While Pepys found Cooper's colouring 'a little forced', his draftsmanship was undoubtedly 'extraordinary'. Pepys resolved to go through with the commission, encouraged by Cooper's tale of how a previous client had failed to pay up. Afterwards, at the coffee house, emerged the double expense of entertaining a glamorous but indebted actor. Hales would indeed paint a portrait of Harris, but Pepys would pay for it.[136]

Within a month, the awful truth about Henry Harris was starting to dawn. One Sunday in April Harris and Banister again came for lunch along with two others. As usual, there was plenty of singing and general merriment. 'But when all was done', reflected Pepys, 'I did begin to think that the pleasure of these people was not worth so often charge and cost to me'. Yet he was too far in to change tack. In the afternoon he went to Hales's house in Holbourn expecting to find Harris sitting for his portrait. No one was in. They were all at the Crown Tavern next

---

[134] Pepys, *Diary*, 6 January 1668 (IX.13). [135] Pepys, *Diary*, 29 March 1668 (IX.138).
[136] Pepys, *Diary*, 30 March 1668 (IX.139-40).

door, listening to stories of suicides. Hales left with Pepys to view progress on the Harris portrait, which promised to be 'pretty like', and 'a very good picture'.[137]

Still Pepys could not keep away. Only three days later he stayed behind after a performance of Etherege's *The Comical Revenge* to see Harris in his dressing room. Groupie-like, Pepys barely got a look in among the 'much company come to him, and the Witts to talk after the play is done and to assign meetings'.[138] In narratives of celebrity, backstage access plays an important role, since it is the sign of what Patricia Meyer Spacks calls 'public intimacy' and 'the illusion of availability', a sign of privileged entry to private space.[139] Although there is more than a suggestion that Pepys was drawn to Harris's distinctive charisma, it is not obvious that either an 'illusion of availability' or what Stella Tillyard describes as the now 'tradable public commodity' of privacy were in play; he was already familiar with Harris, granting him favours and – as his next visit would show – expecting one in return.[140] In May he ventured backstage again to ask Harris for the words to the Echo song in *The Tempest*, Banister having provided him with the tune the week before. Harris duly obliged.[141] But their next encounter showed Pepys that for all his civility and fine conversation, his friend had a seamier side. To the extent that Pepys had a problem with Harris, it was that he was all too available.

On 30 May 1668 he met Harris and others at the New Exchange, a fashionable shopping mall. Along came 'Harry Killigrew, a rogue' who had been banished from Court for spreading lewd rumours about the King's mistress, Lady Castlemaine. Himself hardly innocent of sexual harassment, Pepys was shocked by the group's eagerness to 'take hold of every woman that came by them'. Sitting down to eat, 'mad bawdy talk' prevailed. Why did they speak of 'Ballers', Pepys asked. Harris enlightened him, opening a window into the world of the Restoration libertine. The Ballers were a group of young men who frequented the house of Martha Bennet, a well-known brothel-keeper. There, they danced naked and did 'all the roguish things in the world'. Harris admitted that 'he was among them'. Pepys's closing reflection captures the tensions in his relationship with a man who promised as much as he disappointed: 'what loose company was this that I was in tonight; though full of wit and worth a man's being in it for once, to know the nature of it and their manner

---

[137] Pepys, *Diary*, 26 April 1668 (IX.175).
[138] Pepys, *Diary*, 29 April 1668 (IX.178). Likely features of the leading actors' dressing rooms are described by Judith Milhous and Robert D. Hume, 'Murder in Elizabeth Barry's Dressing Room', *Yale University Library Gazette* 79.3–4 (April 2005), pp. 147–74.
[139] Patricia Meyer Spacks, *Privacy: Concealing the Eighteenth-Century Self* (Chicago: University of Chicago Press, 2003), pp. 2–3.
[140] Stella Tillyard, 'Celebrity in 18th-Century London', *History Today* 55.6 (2005), 20.
[141] Pepys, *Diary*, 11 May 1668 (IX.195).

of talk and lives'.[142] Accordingly, when Pepys saw Hales's finished portrait of Harris, he could not help thinking that the painter had failed to capture the private man he had come to know too well. Probably at Harris's suggestion, Hales had painted him in the role of Orrery's Henry V, an unabashedly noble personage with little of the murky past that colours Shakespeare's character. The picture was 'mighty like a player', and not 'near so good as any yet that he hath made for me'.[143] If Pepys presented Harris with the painting, he did not record the event; and if the painting was not exactly a technical success, it did at least serve to remind Pepys that his friend was, for all his fine conversation and extensive knowledge, a shape-shifter in private as well as on the stage.

Their acquaintance continued. Pepys again found himself inviting Harris to Sunday lunch in July. This time Cooper and Hales were there, as well as the poet Samuel Butler and Richard Reeve, a leading maker of optical instruments. The company pleased Pepys 'mightily – being all eminent men in their way'.[144] In August the two men visited Surgeon's Hall to view the anatomy theatre and a painted panel said to be by Holbein.[145] In his former way, Pepys took the actor to the theatre for a performance of Thomas Shadwell's *The Sullen Lovers*, in which Harris had a pivotal role. Amid a desperately thin audience, one man stood out.

Thomas Shadwell's *The Sullen Lovers* had enjoyed a strong first run of twelve performances in May 1668.[146] By August, interest in it was evidently dwindling, but not from the Earl of Arlington, who with his associates sat conspicuously in an auditorium so empty that Pepys wondered if the play would go ahead at all. *The Sullen Lovers* was the first new play known to have been performed by the Duke's Company under Betterton and Harris's management. The King and the Duke of York attended the premiere, and the play's popularity derived partly from the character role of Sir Positive At-all, a pompous fool who ends up married to a pregnant sex worker (the *Dramatis Personae* of the first edition describes him as 'A foolish Knight, that pretends to understand everything in the World, and will suffer no man to understand anything in his Company'). The role was a satirical portrait of Arlington's enemy, Sir Robert Howard, and it was played by Henry Harris. For those seal commissions, Arlington expected something in return. Impersonation carried risks; in February 1669 the King's Company actor Edward Kynaston was beaten up for imitating Sir Charles Sedley. But Harris's extra jobs brought him more than cash. To have a position at Court, to be commissioned as an engraver by one of the country's most senior ministers, to do his bidding as a theatre manager – these were extra layers of

---

[142] Pepys, *Diary*, 30 May 1668 (IX.218-9).
[143] Pepys, *Diary*, 5 September 1668 (IX.299). The portrait does not appear to have survived.
[144] Pepys, *Diary*, 19 July 1668 (IX.265).   [145] Pepys, *Diary*, 29 August 1668 (IX.293).
[146] Downes, *Roscius Anglicanus*, p. 64.

personal protection in a culture where the very bodies of actors might be as vulnerable as their finances.

5 Managing

Harris became a theatre manager thanks to an entrepreneurial woman. Henrietta Maria du Tremblay adopted the English 'Mary' when she became the third wife of Sir William Davenant. After his death in April 1668 she protected his legacy by arranging for a folio collection of his plays – a tribute their literary merits barely deserved – and by securing the leadership of the Duke's Company. Dual leadership presented obvious risks, not least when one of the parties had been as disloyal as Harris. However, his joint appointment with Betterton confirmed the degree to which the wounds of 1663 had healed. That was not the only consideration. At the time of Davenant's death, Betterton was still off sick, so it was natural to turn to the second most senior actor in the company.

With new leadership came a reorganization of finances and a redistribution of risk. Lady Mary assigned a proportion of her late husband's shares to the principal male actors, making them responsible for operating costs, and Betterton bought out colleagues who did not care for the new arrangements. In Judith Milhous's words, the actor-shareholders were no longer 'carefully sheltered children', but had to adopt a more business-like approach.[147] A further innovation saw Betterton and Harris draw salaries of 20*s* each a week for their new roles. Adding to the cost base, that allowance dented the profits of other shareholders, acting and otherwise, and signalled that company management was not to be taken lightly, either by the managers or the managed. Disciplinary procedures followed against some of the lesser actors. Late in 1669, Matthew Medbourne, a Catholic who was later implicated in the Popish Plot and died for his faith, was sacked and then reinstated.[148] The following year, three others were called to account for repeated absence.[149]

For his first three years in management, Harris appears to have scaled back his acting commitments. In the two and a half years between his appointment in 1668 and the end of the 1669–70 season there is firm evidence of only five new roles, including Sir Positive in Shadwell's *The Sullen Lovers* and Orrery's *Henry V*. Pepys's friend Silas Taylor thought him less than scrupulous when it came to assessing new scripts, on the basis that Harris did not get beyond the first act of Taylor's inauspiciously titled *The Serenade, or Disappointment*.[150] But that was all an experienced actor needed to form a view, and for literary

---

[147] Judith Milhous, *Thomas Betterton and the Management of Lincoln's Inn Fields*, p. 27.
[148] *Document Register* no.540.
[149] *Document Register* nos.554 & 570. The actors were Jeremiah Lisle and two others named only as Adams and Allenson.
[150] Pepys, *Diary*, 7 May 1669 (IX.189).

managers and agents it still is. There was no let up in his Yeoman's duties, with regular court performances and a special showing of Habington's *The Queen of Aragon* for the Duke of York's birthday 'in the guard chamber at St James's'.[151] Since that venue is a rarity among theatrical records of the time, we can assume it needed special fitting out.

Now in his mid-thirties, with guaranteed additional income and a court position, Harris should have been closer than ever to attaining a degree of financial security. Yet at this very time we have found him sponging off Pepys and being pursued for debt by Mary Ingoldsby. The latter problem was almost certainly the trigger for another major development in Harris's life, for it was in 1668 that he separated from his wife Anne.

Anne would later claim that she and her husband had lived together 'quietly and lovingly' for thirteen years following their marriage in 1655. She portrayed herself as a dutiful and respectful wife who sought to maintain a good household. But in 1668 Harris left her without cause, she reported, and ignored her pleas for his return.[152] For his part, he claimed to have received the following advice from the Lord Chief Justice himself: since he was legally liable for his wife's debts, the only way he could evade his wife's creditors, and with them the prospect of detention in a debtor's prison, was to abandon her. He still owed her support, and the amount was precisely what he had gained through co-managing the Duke's Company: 20*s* per week. But it is clear from the Court record that he regularly failed to honour that commitment, sometimes for months at a time. She was, he argued, spending the money on drink. Moreover, he needed to cash to settle her debts with tradesmen named as Mr Allen, a linen draper in Fleet Street, Mr Watkins, a seller of Indian gowns at the Peacock in the Strand, Mr Levett at the Blue Balls in Lincoln's Inn Fields (the implication being that Anne was a customer there too), the vintner at the Globe tavern in Drury Lane, a brewer in St Giles, along with several others.[153]

Anne's assertion that her married life had been quiet and loving was undermined by her other claims about Harris's behaviour during the 1660s. She complained of his libertine lifestyle and of the house parties he had held at great expense (if that was so, Pepys does not appear to have been on the guest list for any of them). She described his subterfuge during the Ingoldsby saga. But when she begrudged his travelling to the Continent to deal in saddles and velvet, she may simply have been referring in part to his duties as Yeoman of the Revels, a role that required him to oversee 'the Apparell a[nd] Trappers of all

---

[151] LS1, p. 147. The performance took place on 14 October 1668. It is not known whether Harris acted in it.
[152] Arches E 6/98. In his own testimony Harris confirmed the date (Arches E 6/138).
[153] See *Document Register* nos.379, 400, 414, 423, 438, 468, 471, 732.

and singular our horses ordained and appointed and hereafter [to] be ordained and appointed for our Iusts and Turneys'.[154] The inconsistencies in her account would eventually count against her.

At the very time when Harris was struggling to keep his wife's creditors at bay, his career took on two new dimensions. The first was yet another job, the second another theatre, in the shape of the new Dorset Garden playhouse. Just before either of those, in May 1670, came an extraordinary episode in his career as both an actor and Yeoman of the Revels. It is an episode that once again bears the fingerprints of his patron, Lord Arlington. John Downes recalled that the company was 'commanded to *Dover,* in *May* 1670', to perform before the King, his sister the Duchess of Orléans, and senior members of the French Court. The two plays were chosen with diplomacy and Arlington's factional interests in mind: Shadwell's *The Sullen Lovers*, giving Harris a further opportunity to make fun of Arlington's enemy Sir Robert Howard; and *Sir Salomon*, a free adaptation of Molière's *L'École des Femmes* by John Caryll, a moderate English Catholic who had written a treatise on the benefits of religious toleration.

Arlington was among the small handful of attendees who knew that the official purpose of the Dover gathering – a new commercial treaty with France – was merely a front. The second, secret treaty committed the King to convert to Catholicism on the promise of French money and military support against the Protestant Dutch and, if needed, his own Parliament and people. In that context, the choice of Caryll's play is telling. *L'École des Femmes* had been a signal success in Paris during the winter of 1662–63, and the first edition was dedicated to none other than the Duchess of Orléans. In Caryll's hands, Molière's comedy of an older man seeking to control the desires of his young fiancée acquires a murkily political flavour. It is an inheritance drama in which the eponymous hero devises secret means to fend off rebellion from the next generation. The threat of tyranny hangs over a play which in the words of Derek Hughes highlights 'arbitrary acts of exclusion: disinheritance, and the denial of education'.[155] Still, it is doubtful whether Charles II ever intended to honour the secret treaty, sympathetic as he was to Arlington and Caryll's moderate and tolerant inclinations.

While it stretches belief to propose that Harris knew what was really going on at Dover, he must have been closely involved in planning the entertainment. As Yeoman of the Revels, he was responsible for fitting out the great hall of Dover Castle. As Arlington's man in the Duke's Company, he would surely have been consulted about suitable repertory for a critically sensitive

---

[154] Grant of office by Charles II to Henry Harris, reproduced in Halliwell-Phillipps, *A Collection of Ancient Documents*, p. 62.

[155] Derek Hughes, *English Drama 1660-1700* (Oxford: Clarendon Press, 1996), p. 119.

diplomatic event. As an actor, his involvement was conventional. In *Sir Salomon* he played the stock, young lover role of Peregrine, who, like Molière's Horace, undoes the hero's marriage plans. Some of Caryll's lines he doubtless spoke with rueful self-consciousness ('it gives me credit for some Mony, which my occasions at present stand in need of').[156] The company did well out of the visit. Where a regular Court performance earned £20, the Dover trip – admittedly more costly – brought in £500.[157] As was often the case, the account was not settled for months, by which time the profit had already been eroded by the death in June 1670 of the Duchess of Orléans, which caused the theatres to close for six weeks.[158]

Conscious that even salaried management was no guarantee of financial security, Harris turned again to his other skills. When Thomas Rawlins died late in 1670, Harris again applied for a role at The Mint. His petition, dated 11 November, states that the 'place of engraver of the seals to his Majesty' had been left 'void' by Rawlins's death. The grant of office bears the same date – possibly a sign that Arlington had intervened to guarantee Harris the role. The document is, however, careful to circumscribe Harris's duties: 'making and engraving the King's signets, arms, seals, &c'. Specifically excluded were other duties associated with the work of The Mint such as coinage and medals.[159] Twenty years on, when Harris became Chief Engraver at The Mint, his skills in that department remained so limited that he had to subcontract the work to the Roettier brothers, paying them from his own salary.[160] As engraver of seals in 1670, he was to be paid £50 a year (perhaps £12,500 in current values), with separate payments for individual seals. He had the opportunity to supplement his income further with private commissions for seal rings and family crests.

Compared to his role as co-manager of the Duke's Company, Harris occupied a lowly rung on The Mint's corporate ladder. A table of salaries dating from the restructure of 1667 depicts a steep hierarchy of roles and pay.[161] Henry Slingsby, the Master-Worker and dining companion of Pepys, drew £500 and the Warden and Comptroller £350 and £300 respectively. The three Roettier brothers claimed £325 between them, while the Surveyor of the Meltings earned £100. Still, what Harris's position lacked in seniority it gained in reliability. Here was a steady second income from a job not prone, like the theatre, to interruption by plague, fire, riot, deaths in the royal family, censorship, or any of the other contingencies that might eat into Duke's Company profit margins. It

---

[156] John Caryll, *Sir Salomon, Or, The Cautious Coxcomb* (London: Henry Herringman, 1671), p. 15.
[157] *Document Register* no.572.
[158] LS1, p. 170. It is possible the Duke's Company was permitted to act in Oxford instead.
[159] *CSPD Domestic, Charles II, 1670. With Addenda, 1660 to 1670*, p. 525.
[160] Challis, *Mint*, p. 364.   [161] Reproduced in Challis, *Mint*, p. 353.

came his way at a time when he was in the process of investing in the expensive new Dorset Garden Theatre and needed to raise all the money he could. There is some evidence that he had already struggled to reconcile the demands of his complex career. On 24 February 1667, Sir James Modyford had written to Arlington's secretary, Joseph Williamson, asking him to 'quicken Mr. Harris' about a 'silver broad seal'.[162]

That seal was for the colony of Providence Island, established by English settlers in 1630 roughly 120 miles off the coast of Nicaragua. Harris had already provided 'Two great seals for Barbados' at a cost of £30 and would be commissioned in 1678 to do likewise for the Leeward Islands. The sequence of events surrounding the Leeward Islands commission suggests that the path to successful completion could be tortuous, and beyond the craftsman's control. On 19 April 1678 Harris gave an undertaking to the Lords committee that he would complete the seal 'within a month at farthest'.[163] Yet it is only in a document dated 21 October 1678 that he was given the design specification for 'two great seals of silver'. The specification was exacting:

> on one side to be engraven our [i.e. the King's] effigies crowned in royal vestments holding a trident in one hand placed sitting on a chariot in the ocean drawn by two sea horses, with the inscription: *Sigillum Insularum S^{ti} Christsophori, Nevis, Antegoa, Montserrat,* &c., on the other sides our arms with the garter, crown, supporters, and mottoes, and this inscription: *Carolus II. Dei Gratia Magna Britanniæ Franciæ at Hiberneæ Rex Fidei Defensor.*[164]

While Harris might be entrusted with such a task – vital if supplies and security measures for the colony were to be authorized – he could not necessarily be trusted to quote fairly for the work. Sir John Ernle, Chancellor of the Exchequer, asked the Master, Henry Slingsby, what he thought would be a reasonable fee, 'the price demanded seeming by the Lords of Trade and Plantations to be too great and unreasonable'. He did, at least, complete the work precisely according to the schedule he had originally promised. On 20 November 1678, Slingsby was deputed to appraise his work. The engraver was still referred to by his main occupation, even though by then he was halfway to leaving it: the seal had been cut, in the words of a letter from a Treasury official, by 'Mr. Harris of the Play House'.[165] Even when that distraction had become a thing of the past, however, Harris's ability to carry out his engraving duties would continue to arouse comment.

---

[162] *CSPD Domestic, 1666-1667*, p. 530.
[163] *CSPD Colonial, America and West Indies, 1669-1674*, p. 242.
[164] *CSPD Colonial, America and West Indies, 1669-1674*, p. 298.
[165] *CSPD Colonial, America and West Indies, 1669-1674*, p. 298.

When he began his new role at The Mint, Harris was already engaged in finding a site for the Duke's Company's next theatre. The playhouse at Lincoln's Inn Fields was cramped and not suited to the latest scenic technology. Along with John Roffey, who in 1662 had bought shares in the company from Davenant, Harris reviewed the options. The Great Fire had created a glut of vacant sites and associated compulsory purchase orders, but the best option came via another Court connection. Just inside the western boundary of the fire zone sat what had been an orchard. Steps down to the river made the journey from Westminster straightforward; a boat was certainly preferable to walking down from Fleet Street, along the Fleet Ditch and past Bridewell Prison. The site belonged to a man who would loom large in Harris's and the company's future. Charles Sackville, 6th Earl of Dorset, was an accomplished poet and, in later years, Lord Chamberlain. In other ways the site was a strange choice. It pushed the company's home eastwards, away from the fast-developing West End and into territory overseen by those who were suspicious of the very idea of public theatres. The Lord Mayor of London himself petitioned against the scheme, but to no avail.[166]

The lease on Dorset Garden was assigned to Harris and Roffey on 11 or 12 August 1670, with a term of thirty-nine years. In theory that would last a lifetime; Betterton had just turned thirty-five and Harris was at least a year older. However, the lease was to be reassigned after four years to two outside investors, who would promptly reassign it again. The annual rent was set at £130 (something like £32,500 in current values) and the shareholders were expected to raise £3000 for construction costs. That turned out to be a drastic underestimate. Carpenters, bricklayers, stonemasons, and glaziers had poured into London for the huge project of rebuilding post-Fire, but the supply of labour still could not cope with demand. Wages rose accordingly, as did the cost of materials. The result was that the Dorset Garden theatre ended up costing three times the original estimate. A newsletter reported that Charles II had helped with a gift of £1000, while a new shareholding scheme closed the remaining gap.[167]

Harris was one of eleven shareholders in the new building. Four were outside investors. The three largest sharers were Lady Davenant, Betterton, and Harris, whose 14 per cent holding entitled him to 19*s* 6*d* every time the company acted.[168] That meant a potential annual return of more than £200 against an initial outlay of £450 per share. It is a measure of Harris's appetite for risk that he was prepared to buy two and a half shares. Perhaps, like Betterton, he funded

---

[166] Richard Baxter, *Reliquiae Baxterianae*, 3 vols (London, 1696), III.89.
[167] For the King's gift, *Document Register* no.657.   [168] *Document Register* no.853.

the purchase partly through borrowing against future income. By the end of 1670 he therefore had five sources to cite as security: acting, co-managing, Yeoman of the Revels, engraver at The Mint, and part-owner of the new theatre. Besides giving him yet another source of income, Dorset Garden reduced his living costs at a time when he had left the family home. He was allowed one of the apartments in the theatre *gratis*, but then charged rent on part of it to the man who ran the orange-selling operation, Richard Middlemore. The apartment would feature in accusations made by Anne Harris, who was slipping behind on rent for her own lodging.[169]

For his part, Harris needed all the security he could get. While the theatre was under construction, performances at the old house in Lincoln's Inn Fields were interrupted for six weeks by another royal death, this time of the Duchess of York, on 31 March 1671.[170] When it came to the choice of an opening play at Dorset Garden, in November that year, the decision was taken not to showcase its new scenic capabilities but to rely instead on two comedy favourites. *Feign'd Innocence* and *The Comical Revenge* had been repertory staples in the 1660s and, from 9 November 1671, brought in the crowds again.[171] Not until the end of November did the company mount a new play, 'all new Cloath'd', in the shape of John Crowne's epic *The History of Charles the Eighth of France*, a stylistic imitation of Dryden's *The Conquest of Granada* whose rhyming couplets stumble and which duly failed to meet expectations; though 'all new Cloath'd', as Downes reported, it 'lasted but 6 Days together, but 'twas Acted now and then afterwards'.[172] Harris had the substantial role of Ferdinand, inheritor of the crown of Naples. Already, it had been necessary to call in the King's Chief Architect, Christopher Wren, to inspect a potentially defective wall.[173] Amid the rush of rebuilding after the Fire, suspicions of poor construction abounded.

Between *Charles VIII* and the end of the 1674–5 season there are signs that Harris's appetite for new roles was flagging further, with only six recorded for that four-year period. With so many other responsibilities, he could do little more than fall back on stock successes such as Warner in *Feign'd Innocence*, Wolsey in *Henry VIII*, Antonio in *The Adventures of Five Hours*, and Sir Frederick in *The Comical Revenge*. Fees for acting in revivals, as well as his building investor income, could see him through. The gain in time was twofold: fewer hours learning new material and fewer mornings rehearsing it. He did, however, maintain a particular loyalty to Thomas Shadwell and Elkanah Settle, who regularly wrote roles for him.

---

[169] *Document Register* no.732. Anne's landlord, Peter Dod, was owed £9 in rent by November 1672.
[170] Lord Chamberlain's order of 1 April 1671, LS1, p. 182.   [171] LS1, pp. 189–90.
[172] Downes, *Roscius Anglicanus,* p. 69.   [173] *Document Register* no.659.

Towards the latter end of that relatively fallow period for new roles came the blizzard of demands related to the production of *Calisto*, an extravagant court masque devised by John Crowne. For a year from December 1674, orders came through for tasks ranging from plastering and glazing to fire shovels and braziers to curtains and seating.[174] The performance required 161 costumes, all of which Harris was tasked with keeping safe 'for his Majesties further Service', in 37 wooden boxes.[175] He was also tasked with maintaining security backstage. The new Lord Chamberlain, Arlington, sent him a list of the sixty or so violinists, dancers, carpenters and other functionaries who alone were to be allowed access.[176] The royal participants, among them the Princesses Mary and Anne, required coaching in their roles.[177]

In the aftermath of *Calisto*, Harris's diet of new roles suddenly accelerated. There were seven in the 1675–6 season. However, by that time he was beginning to scale back on his management responsibilities. Another actor, William Smith, was emerging as a favoured partner for Betterton. Between Harris and Smith there are signs of political difference that would colour the rest of their careers. In 1676, just as Harris was contemplating life away from the responsibilities of managing a theatre company, a long-running domestic issue came to the fore. The crisis that had been brewing for fifteen years took a new turn as his estranged wife Anne began the formal process of suing him.

6 Marital Woes

Harris's patchwork career from the late 1660s onwards can partly be explained with reference to his disastrous marriage. How Anne fared financially after he left her is partly guesswork. His payments to her were at best intermittent, but her brother Richard maintained a business as a goldsmith, in which she appears to have shared. But debts relating to rent and goods had plainly mounted. So, after eight years of separation, hardship and frustration drove her to seek help from a man who exercised dual authority over Henry Harris. The Lord Chamberlain oversaw the workings of the theatre companies via the Office of the Revels. No one was better placed to apply pressure to an actor, theatre manager and Yeoman of the Revels – an adroit move on Anne's part, her understanding of the Lord Chamberlain's role perhaps informed by conversations she had had with her husband. She may even have understood that the Lord Chamberlain since 1674 was someone he knew very well: his de facto patron, Henry Bennet, Earl of Arlington.

---

[174] *Document Register* nos.882 ff. [175] *Document Register* nos.902 & 908.
[176] Reproduced in Boswell, *The Restoration Court Stage*, p. 202.
[177] A detailed account of *Calisto* is available in Boswell, *The Restoration Court Stage*, pp. 177–227.

Whatever pressure Arlington applied to Harris was, in the first instance, decidedly light. Anne first petitioned for maintenance on 25 January 1676.[178] For nearly two years Harris held out. Only on 8 November 1677 did Anne begin to make progress. If her husband did not settle, she was granted 'free Leave to take her course against him according to ye rules of these Courts'.[179] The institution in question was the Court of Arches, the highest ecclesiastical court in the Province of Canterbury. Since Harris did not respond to the petition of 8 November 1677, the case went to court on 1 December. Records of the case do not specify the basis of Anne's claim. Whether she was merely trying to secure a ruling on maintenance or requesting an order for Harris to resume cohabitation (which lay within the court's power) is not clear. What is plain is that money and accusations of abuse – both verbal and physical – feature prominently in the account.

Harris probably drew on connections and financial resources to employ the best possible counsel. His representative, Everard Exton, had been a proctor of the court since 1663 and came from a prominent legal family, with a father who had been a Judge in the Court of Admiralty and a brother who in time would become Dean of the Court of Arches. Anne, by contrast, had to rely on Thomas Champante, a novice with only a year's experience of the court. Still, Exton's initial moves failed. In February 1678 he tried to have the case dismissed on the grounds of immunity: Harris was a royal servant and as such, he argued, enjoyed protection. Numerous other cases said otherwise, however, and even the Arlington connection was no help.

Anne opened her case by describing her family circumstances and the early years of her marriage. She admitted that in her desperation to raise money she had pawned the deeds of the marital home in The Strand and taken in lodgers. Observing her 'civill carriage and behaviour', the lodgers treated her, she claimed, as a companion rather than a landlady. She even recalled that the Countess of Carnarvon had received her as a guest at her home near Leighton Buzzard.[180] By contrast, Anne portrayed Henry at the time of their marriage as 'a person of a pore and meane condicion', the son of an indigent scale maker who was worth little and frequently driven to pawn what goods he possessed. Henry himself, being 'profuse and addicted to extravagansie', ran up debts which Anne's mother had to pay. He was unable, she alleged, to maintain his wife at that time without relief from her family. He had funded his ventures to the Continent to sell horses and saddles by pawning her best gown and petticoat

---

[178] *Document Register* no.956.   [179] *Document Register* no.1029.
[180] Arches Ee 4 ff. 581r-588v. Apparently a reference to Elizabeth Dormer, née Capel (1633–1678), wife of Charles Dormer, 2nd Earl of Carnarvon. The Countess was unfortunately (or perhaps conveniently) dead by the time Anne Harris gave her testimony.

as well as the family plate. As though that were not bad enough, he had purloined most of the rings and other goods from her goldsmith's shop. Anne was left behind in a pitiful condition, and but for her family's intervention, she testified, she might have starved.[181]

Then the Dorset Garden theatre entered her account. Harris was still lodging there, she said, opposite the apartment occupied by another senior actor, Cave Underhill.[182] It became the scene for bitter quarrels over money. Anne would invoke the needs of their daughter. She claimed that Harris withheld her allowance for months at a time; she described visits to his playhouse lodgings when, 'ready to starve', she entreated him on her knees for help, only to be told to 'live per your witts you bitch'. Taking him at his word, Anne then stole his tankard, selling it after Henry had told her to 'keep, it and sell it and be hanged you bitch'. On a further mission she claimed to have found Henry just back from one of his debauches. He allegedly fell upon her, beat her, pulled her down the stairs by the hair and one leg, stamped on her amid the stage scenery, and tore her clothes. On another occasion she went armed with an 'ivory busk' (that is, a whalebone used for stiffening corsets) and struck him on the lips as he crammed her against a wheel then beat her on the head and face with his slipper. She admitted she had injured him ('I have marked him for my rogue'), but admitted he was still able to rehearse that morning and act in the afternoon.[183]

Harris responded with a character assassination of his own. Dismissing her claims about her father's status, he stated that he had treated Anne lovingly and kindly during the early years of their marriage, providing for her and living comfortably with her until – the accusation that coloured and perhaps determined the outcome of the case – she became addicted to drink. Helplessly, embarrassingly, scandalously under the influence, she would scold him in public so that he could no longer endure her company. He further alleged that she had defrauded him to fund her addiction. She would pawn his clothes and steal his money; once she swapped coins in a bag with stones of the same weight. During the plague year of 1665 she procured a key to his cabinet so that she might pawn some pearl necklaces and a gold watch set with diamonds. She had also run up debts for which he, as her husband, was by law responsible, and for which he had been arrested and sued.[184] He claimed to have been so distracted by her conduct that he was barely able to work; so impoverished had he become thanks to her excesses that he was 'not worth a groat'. Making that claim, he conveniently skated over the impact of plague and fire in the lead up to their separation. The only way to avoid imprisonment for debt, he claimed

---

[181] Arches Ee 4 ff. 581r-588v. [182] Arches Eee 6 ff. 399v-400r.
[183] Arches Ee 4 ff. 581r-588v. [184] See n.153.

on the Lord Chief Justice's authority, was to abandon her.[185] It is not at all clear that those were accepted grounds for desertion.[186]

For witnesses Henry produced two fellow actors of the Duke's Company. His choice of a subordinate and an old friend naturally raises suspicions. The first was Joseph Williams, aged about nineteen in 1678. Williams testified that he had known Henry and Anne for roughly six years and had been Henry's apprentice or servant before taking to the stage. At pains to emphasize his impartiality, Williams swore that he was 'far from depending on Harris' and had no fear of being ejected from his position at the theatre, which at that point earned him £30 a year. He even stated that Harris had opposed his joining the company in the first place and barely acknowledged his presence whenever they came across each other.[187] Williams's evidence against Anne was nevertheless damaging.

He claimed that she 'often besotted herself much with intemperate drinking of strong drink and brandy, strong waters and such violent liquors' – something of an irony since Williams himself was later said to 'love his bottle better than his business'.[188] While drunk, Anne had been outrageously abusive toward her husband; she had even 'flown' at him and struck him. Williams swore that he had himself delivered the twenty shillings per week Henry provided for maintenance, but Anne was never satisfied. In response to a question from Anne as to whether Henry frequented loose and infamous women, brought them home to his lodging, and then entertained them all night, Williams admitted seeing women with Henry in his apartment, but claimed they were merely applying for employment in the theatre (it is hard not to detect a euphemism for the particular kind of exploitation now referred to as a 'casting couch' culture).[189]

The second witness was Cave Underhill, Harris's colleague and neighbour. However, Underhill testified only that he had known Henry and Anne as a couple for thirteen or fourteen years and had often visited them at home. He thought they might have continued to live together comfortably but for Anne's turbulent temper. While lodging at the theatre he had often witnessed her railing at Henry, calling him 'you rogue, you dogg, you pitiful raskill, get you to your

---

[185] Arches E 6/138 and Ee 4 ff. 560v-562r. The Lord Chief Justice at the time Harris referred to was Sir John Kelynge, who served between 1665 and his death in 1671. Kelynge had a mixed record of service. He was often the subject of complaints and threats of impeachment; see Eric Stockdale, 'Sir John Kelynge, Chief Justice of the King's Bench 1665-1671', Bedfordshire Historical Records Society 59 (1980), pp. 43–53.

[186] See Rebecca Probert, *Marriage Law and Practice in the Long Eighteenth Century: A Reassessment* (Cambridge, 2009).

[187] Arches Eee 6 f. 399r.   [188] Cibber, *Apology*, p. 138.

[189] Arches Eee 6 ff. 397v-399r; for Anne's questions or 'interrogatories', E 6/96.

whores you rogue ... ' Her tormenting abuse could only, Underhill concluded, disquiet and injure Harris both personally and professionally.[190]

Anne's witnesses did her no more favours than her representation by an inexperienced proctor. Dr Nathan Paget spoke for the support Anne's family had provided, describing her upbringing as strict and proper, but nine of those she named failed to appear.[191] They included Harris's elder brother John, Martha Bennet the sex worker, and Lady Mary Davenant, doubtless named because of the power she exercised over Harris as a senior shareholder in the Duke's Company, and for her recollections of his disloyalty in 1663.[192] Lady Mary's name would resurface later in the case, but not to Anne's advantage.

Anne also called three witnesses from the Duke's Company. She needed Thomas Betterton, Henry's co-manager, and Alexander Davenant, who kept the accounts, to give evidence concerning Henry's income. In every other respect they may as well have appeared for her husband. Under questioning, they repeated Harris's accusations of her drunkenness and profligacy. Betterton had the reputation, in Colley Cibber's words, of being 'a man of veracity', and his own marriage appears to have been a model of contentment.[193] Worse still was Anne's choice of William Peare, a man in his early thirties who had worked in the theatre for sixteen years, initially as a servant to Henry. He had lived with the couple at Scroop's Court and witnessed their quarrels, which he duly blamed on Anne. Peare was also the dogsbody who fetched the goods that drove them into debt; along with Williams, he was tasked with delivering the twenty shillings per week Henry provided for Anne after their separation. Such was her lack of responsibility, Peare claimed, that no sooner was one maintenance payment made than she would demand another.[194]

Betterton and Davenant did at least provide a full account of the income Henry Harris derived from the Duke's Company. They identified four streams: (i) for his acting, he received a tenth share of the profits of the theatre; (ii) for half an adventurer's (i.e. investor's) share, which he had purchased for £200, he received the equivalent of a fortieth share of the profits (it seems he had already sold the additional two shares he bought when the playhouse was being built); (iii) he received rental income from the theatre building, having invested £1200 towards

---

[190] Arches Eee 6 ff. 399r-400r.   [191] Arches Eee 6 ff. 336r-337v.
[192] Others who failed to appear were George Moore, Elizabeth Dutton, John Wallis, Nathaniel Redding, William Ward, and a man named only as 'Lee' (Arches A 13 ff. 66r, 118r). That man may have been the playwright, Nathaniel Lee, a man whose unstable temperament would have made him a problematic witness; during the period of Anne's lawsuit, in September 1678, Harris appeared as Tiresias in Lee and Dryden's *Oedipus*.
[193] Cibber, *Apology*, p. 98. For Betterton's marriage to Mary Saunderson see Roberts, *Thomas Betterton*, pp. 90–92; the marriage lasted 47 years.
[194] Arches Eee 6 ff. 336r-342v, 344r-345r.

its construction; and (iv), he drew a salary for his role as co-manager. Impressive though that list might seem, Henry had a point when he argued that shares of profits in the theatre were very uncertain. A play might, after all, lose money. Alexander Davenant recorded that, for his one-tenth acting share and half an adventurer's share, Harris received £44 7d in 1675; £230 10s 2d in 1676; and £187 6s 4d in 1677, up to November 30 that year. For the rent from his share of the building he received £220 8s 3d in 1675; £236 15s 6d in 1676; and £219 9s in 1677, again up to November 30. For his role as co-manager he received £38 3s 4d in 1675, and £22 in 1676 'for as much of the year as it continued'. After November 1677, Davenant testified, all income was reduced because the theatre was in debt to tradesmen to the tune of over £1200. It had been agreed that the debt would be paid out of the profits. In the months between then and April 1678, Harris therefore received little from his acting and adventurer's shares.[195] His other roles, as Engraver at The Mint and Yeoman of the Revels, do not feature in Betterton and Davenant's list, although they must have known about them.

Cases often lingered in the Court of Arches for a number of years and frequently never arrived at a judgement. In *Harris vs Harris* all relevant evidence had been presented by the end of 1678, with the case seemingly ready for conclusion. The initiative, however, lay with the parties concerned. Anne, the plaintiff, lay low for a while, perhaps nervous that the cards were stacked against her. Not until May 1680 did she come back to court with an unsuccessful attempt to introduce further evidence against her husband.[196] After yet another hiatus she appeared again, on June 8, 1681, to complain that Henry was withholding the alimony assigned by the court for the duration of the case.[197] Henry's response came on June 25, when his proctor produced three exhibits, lodged earlier in the court registry. The first was a letter from Anne to Lady Mary Davenant, beginning 'Madam, I hope you have had your foul desire of my husband . . . ' Presumably Henry was confident it could not be proved he had enjoyed a sexual relationship with Lady Davenant, but aimed instead to portray his wife as a jealous and paranoid woman. Exhibit two was a letter from Anne to Henry which ended, 'Curse light on you is the Prayer of your Wife'. The third was a diatribe against Henry put into circulation by Anne which began, 'My Deare pretty Puppy of a Panch-gutted Rascall' (now in his late forties, Harris was evidently showing signs of middle-aged spread); the same piece ended, 'I will now laugh at my selfe for shedding a Teare to soe poore a cheating lying thieving Rogue'. Anne did not deny her authorship of the three documents. Unfortunately only the opening and concluding words of each are

---

[195] Arches Eee 6 ff. 341v-342v (Betterton), 344r-345r (Davenant).   [196] Arches A 14 f. 253v.
[197] Arches A 15 f. 101.

now preserved in the records, but it appears the three items helped colour the outcome of the case. Sentence was pronounced on the same day.[198]

That task fell to Sir Robert Wiseman (c.1610–1684), Dean of the Arches since 1672 and a noted jurist.[199] He found decisively in Henry's favour. Anne's case was dismissed as defective and lacking foundation. She was, Wiseman pronounced, a bad, tempestuous woman, unsuitable to live with Henry as his wife.[200] He did at least award her a grant of alimony, of fifteen shillings a week, less than the twenty shillings which Henry was reported to have paid since their separation, but with the merit of relative security.[201] Nevertheless, the deduction of five shillings smacks of retribution – the imposition, perhaps, of temperance via the purse.

Anne Harris's case against her husband does not speak well of the way the Court of Arches dealt with female plaintiffs. That much gives no cause for surprise. More elusive are the questions the case raises about the social status of actors at a time when money, property and land were, according to well-established narratives, beginning to cede ground as qualifying criteria to manners and wit.[202] Class was self-evidently a weapon in Anne and Henry's attacks on each other. Where he characterized her as a mere carter's daughter, she sought to replace his glamorous public image with that of a lowly scale maker. When Judge Wiseman ruled that Anne was not a suitable companion for her husband, one implication was that Henry should be considered a notch or two above her. Had the judge been of the same mind as the scabrous Robert Gould, poet and disappointed playwright, he might have concluded that Harris's current profession marked him out as a natural companion for the 'bad, tempestuous' Anne. Actors were, in Gould's words,

> A pack of idle, pimping, sponging slaves,
> A miscellany of rogues, fools and knaves;
> A nest of lechers, worse than Sodom bore
> And justly merit to be punished more:
> Diseased, in debt, and every moment dunn'd;
> By all good Christians loath'd, and their own kindred shunn'd.[203]

---

[198] Arches A 15 f. 115r.
[199] Wiseman was the author of an important legal text, *The Law of Lawes, or, The Excellency of Civil Law above All Other Humane Laws Whatsoever* (London, 1664).
[200] Arches B 10/54: 'Annam Harris fuisse et esse feminam turbulentam variis modis improbam et cum dicto Henrico Harris conjugaliter vivere inidoneam pronuntiamus.'
[201] The alimony was also less than the twenty shillings awarded to Anne at the start of the case in 1677 (ten shillings for her and ten for Henrietta Harris for as long as she was in the custody of her mother). Henrietta was probably of age and no longer with Anne by 1681.
[202] See, for example, Paul Langford, *A Polite and Commercial People: England 1727-1783* (Oxford: Clarendon Press, 1989).
[203] Robert Gould, 'A Satyr against the Play-house', in his *Poems, Chiefly Consisting of Satyrs and Satirical Epistles* (London, 1689), p. 186.

Not an unfair description of Henry Harris, one might think. Yet in the Court of Arches the actor had perhaps conducted himself in the way admired by Pepys when he spotted him at the coffee house with Dryden 'and all the wits of the town', engaged in 'very witty and pleasant discourse'. His 'curious understanding' and 'fine conversation' continued to impress Pepys even as they vied for supremacy in his mind with Harris's roistering at the Blue Balls. As much as his networks, the actor's personal accomplishments counted in his favour when pitched against those of a woman unused to the business of performance. A trained memory alone gave him a further advantage. His stage presence was not, like Betterton's, built on grandeur or intensity of emotion, but on easy charm and the uncanny ability to improvise he had shown in Sir William Davenant's *The Rivals* when he rescued Winifred Gosnell from her own tunelessness.[204]

A bitter irony for Anne was the credibility of one of her key witnesses. She had called Thomas Betterton for his knowledge of theatre finances, but his refusal to endorse her wider account of her marriage made him an ideal character witness for her husband. No one could have presented a more respectable appearance. His connections were, like Harris's, elevated. He was apparently on good terms with John Tillotson, Fellow of the Royal Society and from 1694 Archbishop of Canterbury.[205] He befriended the MP and amateur playwright, Richard Norton, whose country home he visited.[206] He even corresponded with Thomas Thynne, Viscount Weymouth, about their respective art collections.[207] Whatever their sometime professional differences, Betterton and Harris shared an experience Anne could only dream of: a lasting connection with the upper echelons of London society. The two men had, after all, spent the best part of a decade co-managing the Duke's Company, where in Judith Milhous's words it had fallen to Harris to carry out 'the socializing which made important friends for the theatre at Court'.[208] That was not, to use a colloquialism, mere schmoozing, but integral to business. They might be called on to arrange performances before royalty at Whitehall or Windsor or, as with *Calisto*, make arrangements for royalty themselves to perform.

It has been argued that the growing industry of salacious gossip about actors' private lives was designed to offset the threat constituted by their

---

[204] See earlier, n.101.
[205] George Whitefield, *The Works of the Reverend George Whitefield*, 7 vols. (London, 1771-2), IV.339.
[206] John Le Neve, *The Lives and Characters of the Most Illustrious Persons British and Foreign* (London, 1713), pp. 534–5.
[207] Roberts, frontispiece to *Thomas Betterton*.
[208] Milhous, *Thomas Betterton and the Managament of Lincoln's Inn Fields*, p. 30.

performances of gentility on the stage.[209] That seems more true of actresses than of their male counterparts. The suit of Anne Harris against her wayward husband certainly suggests that the performance of gentility might serve actors singularly well whether they were on stage or off it. In this particular case, the performance was evidently so convincing that it convinced even a distinguished judge in the Court of Arches that, for all the frantic business and debauchery of Henry Harris's life beyond the theatre, it was no performance at all, but the real thing.

7 Last Years

While the Arches case was proceeding, Harris's theatrical career was unravelling. His decision to give up management completely in 1678 may have been financially motivated. He could, after all, turn his hand to a variety of trades that might yield a more secure income in less time. The theatre was, besides, edging towards the precipice of the Popish Plot years, when audiences were lean and serious violence might break out.[210] Harris's connections remained sound and his lifestyle unchanged: in June 1678 it was said that Charles Sackville, 6th Earl of Dorset, was unwell 'for he drinkes aile with Shadwell & Mr Haris at the Dukes house all day long'.[211] The connection with Dorset makes it plausible that a mere actor should have received his legal advice that year from the Lord Chief Justice. It is likely too that Harris was growing increasingly disenchanted with life as a servant of the Catholic Duke of York. Both Dorset and Shadwell had impeccable Protestant credentials (Dorset would become William III's Lord Chamberlain), while Harris's replacement as co-manager, William Smith, was a favourite of the Duke's who joined the Jacobite army in 1689.

Two reports link Harris to the machinations of the Duke of York's rival during the Succession Crisis that gripped Parliament between 1678 and 1683. James Scott, Duke of Monmouth, was Charles II's illegitimate son, backed as Protestant successor by the Whig party. Harris and Monmouth had known each other since the 1660s. Among Harris's early assignments as Yeoman of the Revels was making arrangements for a court masque in February 1665 in which Monmouth and his wife were among twelve dancers.[212] For the performance of *Sir Salomon Single* at Dover in 1670, it was Monmouth who intervened as Yeoman, providing James Nokes with out-size props that

---

[209] E.g. Dawson, *Gentility and the Comic Theatre of Late Stuart London*, pp. 217–38.

[210] See, for example, the incident at Dorset Garden reported in George Parker's *The True News; or, Mercurius Anglicanus*, 4-7 February 1680, when 'some Gentlemen in their Cupps entring into the Pitt, flinging Links at the Actors, and using several reproachfull speeches against the Dutchess of P[ortsmouth] and other persons of Honour, which has occasioned a Prohibition from farther Acting'.

[211] Report by Nell Gwyn, *Document Register* no.1056.

[212] Pepys, *Diary*, 3 February 1665 (VI.29).

mocked the latest French fashions (Downes recalled that Nokes kept the Duke's sword 'until his dying day').[213] Harris's theatrical connection with Monmouth continued with the 1675 court masque *Calisto*, where the Duke once again performed.

In June 1683, Monmouth's agitation for the Crown forced him into hiding; in July, he was charged with high treason. The hunt was on. Sir Roger L'Estrange sent Secretary of State Leoline Jenkins a report of suspicious activity around a house in Russell Street owned by 'Mrs. Nedham, the Duke of Monmouth's miss'. All the shutters were closed, and L'Estrange's man made note of a back door. Nedham was 'observed to give a kind of signal knock at the door and was immediately admitted', while 'a suspicious person was seen coming early from Tottenham Court'. A more familiar face was easily identified: 'Harris, the player, a venomous fellow, and another as bad as himself'.[214] In theory, that venomous fellow might have been Joseph Harris, an actor in the newly formed United Company, but for an anonymous tip off on 13 July 1683 that Monmouth was rumoured to be hiding at either Drury Lane or Dorset Garden, where Harris continued to rent an apartment.[215]

Between James II's accession in 1685 and his downfall in 1688, there is no evidence of Harris's work as an engraver. If he did not lose his post entirely, he was made to suffer through a lack of commissions. Nevertheless, he showed sufficient political acumen – not to mention determination in the face of diminishing income streams – to continue as Yeoman of the Revels. A document from 1687 specifies the sum of £73 to be paid to 'Henry Harris, gent., Yeoman of the Revels', presumably with reference to the fitting out of the court theatre over the Christmas period; payments to carpenters continued until May 1687, while in June a payment was made for 'mending ye cloth of ye clouds'.[216] James II remained a keen playgoer, largely at court and occasionally at the public playhouse. Records survive of 46 performances between May 1685 and May 1687 that were attended by the King either at the public theatres or – in 32 of those cases – at Whitehall.[217] The Yeoman's responsibility to facilitate 'Masques, Revells and Disguisings' made Harris a familiar and even conspicuous figure at court during that period. His previous association with the Duke's Company made him an effective go-between and was enough to provide at least a mask of loyalty.

One particular court performance stands out. On 10 October 1685 there was what Samuel Pepys described as 'a mighty Musique-Entertainment at Court for

---

[213] Downes, *Roscius Anglicanus*, p. 64.   [214] *CSPD* 1 Jan to 30 June 1683, p. 372.
[215] *CSPD* 29/428 no. 108; *Document Register* no.1212.
[216] *Calendar of Treasury Books, 1685-1689*, VIII.III.1456; *Document Register* nos.1303 & 1307.
[217] Reproduced in Allardyce Nicoll, *Restoration Drama 1660-1700*, pp. 312–313.

the welcoming home the King and Queen'. The occasion therefore partly marked the success of royal forces in quashing Monmouth's rebellion in July 1685, with the subsequent quasi-judicial campaign known as the Bloody Assizes, when hundreds of rebel corpses were displayed across the south west of England. Though loyally installed as James's Second Secretary of the Navy (a post he lost when William came to the throne three years later), Pepys was unimpressed by the script. Bemoaning the frequency of the words 'Arms, Beauty, Triumph, Love, Progeny, Peace, Dominion, Glory, &c', he thought the 'Poet-Prophet' had sought out more 'Rhimes than Reasons'.[218]

The identity of the Poet-Prophet is not known, and the script has not survived. The job would normally have fallen to John Dryden, Poet Laureate and Harris's old acquaintance. But Dryden's pleasure in writing royal celebrations had been dimmed by his experience, in the winter of 1684–5, of working with the French composer Louis Grabu on *Albion and Albanius*, an extravaganza celebrating the achievements of Charles II and his royal brother. The poet compared the experience to being 'bound 'Prentice to some doggerel Rhymer, who makes Songs to Tunes'.[219] A likely alternative to Dryden was the rather less gifted John Crowne, author of the 1675 court masque, *Calisto*, a favourite of James, and a writer with experience of hanging on to Dryden's coat tails. Two of Crowne's plays, *Sir Courtly Nice* and *City Politiques*, feature in the list of 32 Whitehall performances; in April 1688, James would attend the author benefit night of the same dramatist's *Darius, King of Persia*.[220]

Crowne and Harris had been familiar since the early 1670s, their acquaintance book-ended by a pair of Roman Catholic clerics. In one of the last new plays the Duke's Company gave at Lincoln's Inn Fields in 1671, Harris had played a scheming, drunken cardinal who has usurped the throne of Poland (eventually he is forced to commit suicide via a poisoned handkerchief). Given what we know of Harris's involvement in reviewing new plays, it is possible that he introduced *Juliana, or The Princess of Poland*, and its author, to the company. It was Crowne who was entrusted with writing the company's first new play to be performed at the Dorset Garden theatre, *The History of Charles the Eighth of France*.[221] The next play of Crowne's in which it is certain Harris had a role was dedicated to Harris's ally Dorset (then merely Charles, Earl of Middlesex). In *The Countrey Wit* Harris appeared in the cameo role of Merry,

---

[218] R.G. Howard, ed., *Letters and the Second Diary of Samuel Pepys* (London, 1932), cited in LS1, p. 343. For an account of doubts about James's policies in Pepys's circle, see Richard Ollard, *Pepys. A Biography* (Oxford: Oxford University Press, 1984), pp. 285–7.
[219] Cited in Winn, *John Dryden and His World*, p. 394.
[220] Nicoll, *Restoration Drama 1660-1700*, pp. 312–313; Letter from Lord Granville to Sir William Leveson, 5 May 1688 cited in LS1, p. 363.
[221] See earlier, n.172.

chipper servant of 'a wild young Gentleman of the Town' played by Betterton (by now, presumably, he felt more relaxed about being the great man's sidekick).[222] Harris's last known role was in another Crowne play, as another scheming Cardinal, this time the illegitimate son of John of Gaunt. Crowne's prologue ends with the hope that the audience will relish 'A little Vinegar against the *Pope*', and the play is an unashamedly partisan piece of anti-Catholic propaganda written in the wake of the Popish Plot. The Cardinal's set piece soliloquy in Act 2 blends anti-papal vitriol with grudging complaints drawn from Edmund's musings in *King Lear*.[223]

If Pepys made the 'mighty Musique-Entertainment' of October 1685 sound like an attempt to reproduce the platitudinous grandeur of *Albion and Albanius*, his reference to the 'Poet-Prophet' suggests private doubts as to whether a reign built on the brutal divisiveness of James's world view could possibly bring lasting 'Beauty, Triumph, Love, Progeny, Peace, Dominion' or 'Glory'. Harris, drinking buddy of the Earl of Dorset, stuck to the business of commissioning materials and performers. Readying the Whitehall theatre for such an entertainment required the tightest of tight-lipped diplomacy.

His last known brush with theatrical matters raises a question about his personal sense of allegiance. In 1695 he was proposed as joint intermediary with William Smith when Betterton and his colleagues resolved to break free of the management of Christopher Rich.[224] What is curious about the proposal is that it was Rich, Betterton's dire enemy, who made it. A long association with Betterton suggests that Harris might have been thought biased in favour of his former colleague. But Rich, a man wary of putting any adversary at an advantage, perhaps knew that Harris did not feel that way. He may even have sensed that as Harris grew into his sixties and saw Betterton continuing to draw the crowds and confirm his legendary status as the most successful actor of his time, some of the old resentment from the strike of 1663 had returned. Such moral suppleness was, after all, no more than one might expect from the friend of Dorset who worked at the Court of James II, or the libertine who occasionally appalled Pepys (or the 'ayery' type reported to him), or the wife-beater who got off at the Court of Arches, or the 'venomous fellow' under surveillance by a government spy.

---

[222] John Crowne, *The Countrey Wit* (London: James Magnes and Richard Bentley, 1675), np.
[223] Crowne, *Henry the Sixth with the Murder of Humphrey, Duke of Gloucester* (London: R. Bentley and M. Magnes, 1681), p. 17.
[224] Submission of the Patentees [i.e. Charles Killigrew, Sir Thomas Skipwith and Christopher Rich] to the Lord Chamberlain, 19 and 22 March 1695, LC 7/3, fols.62-3; cited in *Document Register* no.1498.

It took the accession of William III for Harris's former portfolio career to be revived in earnest. In 1690 he succeeded George Bowers as Chief Engraver to the Mint, a post that came with the handsome salary of £325. Bowers' tenure had been brief in the extreme – a mere three months – and Harris moved quickly amid fluid circumstances. There had already been turnover in the engraving department. Joseph and Philip Roettier had left for Paris and Brussels respectively, while their elder brother John was training up his sons, James and Norbert, to succeed him. It was James and Norbert Roettier who created William III's new great seal, as well as the dies for the coronation medal and the fresh issue of gold and silver coins.[225] The younger Roettiers were as clearly Harris's superior in craft as the elder had been. They were also Catholics. By guile, long association, and probably by dint of friendship with the Earl of Dorset – drinking buddy, Lord Chamberlain, and ardent Williamite – Harris replaced Bowers.

He knew he was not quite up to the job. Immediately, he agreed with James and Norbert that they would do most of the work. From his handsome new salary of £325 Harris therefore kept only £125 a year, giving the remainder, plus payments for piece work, to his younger colleagues. Norbert stayed for five years before leaving for France. James was less fortunate. In 1697 he was fired. Business at The Mint had long defied proper accountability; poor record-keeping was rife and there were continual stories of clipping and counterfeiting. When a Commons committee looked into the matter, Harris testified that 'dies that are within the Tower' had been used to create illegal currency and that James Roettier had prevented him from inspecting the facility where the dies were kept.[226] Roettier's Catholicism counted against him. Nevertheless, he was permitted to keep such tools as were not used for coinage and maintained a source of an income from an annuity his father had bought in 1669. Still lacking the skills normally required of a Chief Engraver, Harris turned to further migrant labour in the shape of John Croker, a German jeweller, for assistance with coinage.[227] Those changes must have come to the attention of the man who for the past year had been Warden of the Mint, Isaac Newton, praised for his vigorous prosecution of fraudsters.[228]

Even when it came to Harris's specialism, the cutting of royal seals, there is evidence of official dissatisfaction with the speed and accuracy of his work. A report to the Council of Trade and Plantations dated 9 March 1698 complains

---

[225] Challis, *Mint*, pp. 363–4.   [226] Challis, *Mint*, p. 364.   [227] Challis, *Mint*, pp. 364–5.
[228] Challis, *Mint*, p. 392. For all his diligence, Newton was initially surprised and discouraged by the scale of The Mint's problems. It had been offered to him as a sinecure, but in 1697, one year after his appointment, he asked to be released. The request was declined, and he carried on for a further two and a half years.

that the seals for Virginia and Bermuda carried the names of previous monarchs, while the one for New Hampshire had no name at all. Harris was ordered to explain in person.[229] In May of the same year he was asked to confirm the designs for the Bermuda and New Hampshire seals, presumably by way of reassurance that earlier errors would not be repeated. Harris's reply survives in summary form:

> both seals were engraved with the King's arms, garter, supporters, motto and crown, with the inscriptions, Sigil: Insular: Nostra: de Bermud: in Americ. for Bermuda; and Sigil: Provinciae Nostrae Nov: Hamptoniæ in Americ:[230]

On 17 June he received an official reminder to dispatch the seals for Virginia and Maryland; a further commission covered Massachusetts Bay.[231]

By now, Harris was approaching seventy and showing signs of fatigue. In June 1702, asked to prepare drawings for 'Seals for the Plantations', he replied, as though with a sigh, that he would do the work 'with what dispatch he c[ould]'.[232] He did not live to finish his final commission in the service of empire. On 24 October 1704 Henry Furness asked for the Council's directions as to completing the work begun by Harris, whom he described as his grandfather.

What is known of Harris's private life in his later years is limited to the terms of a will dated the day before his death in 1704. Henry left his whole estate, including houses in London, Middlesex, and elsewhere, in trust for Elizabeth Furness, the wife of George Furness of London, a merchant, and their three children.[233] Elizabeth was required to complete work on seals left unfinished by Henry and it has been assumed that she was his daughter.[234] However, it is telling that Henry never described or acknowledged her as such in his will. She was clearly not the daughter of Henry and Anne since she is not mentioned in the Arches case, and the dates of birth of her children, Henry (1695), Elizabeth (1696), and George (1701) suggest that she herself may have been born after Henry and Anne had separated.[235] The Arches case removed any possibility that Anne could again cohabit with Henry. She may simply have died in its aftermath, while no trace has survived of her daughter Henrietta, or for that matter of

---

[229] *CSPD Colonial, America and West Indies, 1697-1698*, p. 127.
[230] *CSPD Colonial, America and West Indies, 1697-1698*, p. 190.
[231] *CSPD Colonial, America and West Indies, 1697-1698*, pp. 274 & 743.
[232] *CSPD Colonial, America and West Indies, 1697-1698*, p. 380.
[233] National Archives PROB 11/478/80. Given Henry's experience of marriage, it is unsurprising that he stipulated that George Furness was not to intermeddle or receive any part of the bequest to his wife.
[234] Challis, 'Henry Harris', p. 428.
[235] Henry and Elizabeth were christened at St. Peter le Poer in Old Broad Street, London, respectively on 20 June 1695 and 9 June 1696. George was christened at St. Paul Covent Garden on 21 July 1701.

any remarriage for Henry. Elizabeth Furness may well, therefore, have been his illegitimate child.[236] Whatever the case, by 1694 Henry Harris and the Furness family, three generations, were living together in Charles Street West, in the parish of St. Paul's, Covent Garden, where Henry was buried in 1704.[237] His wayward life had, it seems, reached a quiet conclusion.

For theatre historians, Harris's life is unsettling for reasons that go beyond his moral shortcomings. Although the Greenhill portrait of him as Wolsey suggests he came to be associated – perhaps by his own choice – with Cardinal roles, the range of parts he took on suggests that attributing 'lines' or character types to Restoration actors can underestimate the variety of their work on stage, and the degree to which they could control the type of parts they played.[238] While it is true that some performers clearly had roles written for them (Thomas Otway's for Elizabeth Barry spring to mind), Harris had to be just as supple and adaptive on the stage as he was off it. Warriors, schemers, lovers, sidekicks, libertines, kings, potentates, politicians, gossips, and philosophers all feature in his list of known roles, which traversed tragedy, comedy, history, pastoral, in each case both ancient and modern.[239] Such evidence as we possess of speaking styles during the period equally suggests a diversity of practice depending on genre and individual style.[240]

If we consider only Harris's career as an actor, the question arises of what it meant to have such a 'career' – supposing that term is not anachronistic – in the late seventeenth century. In the now vanished world of nineteenth- and twentieth-century repertory theatre, gifted performers emerged from drama school, stepped into minor roles, and depending on talent eventually gained the chance to play the great classical roles, graduating from one tragic hero to the next in a process determined by biology: young Hamlet to mature Macbeth to old Lear and corpulent Falstaff. We might discern such a pattern in the career of Thomas Betterton, with the caveat that Betterton was still playing young Hamlet at the age of seventy-four. After his bid to become 'equal with

---

[236] No further information on Elizabeth has come to light apart from her will, proved in 1732, where she is described as a widow, of Hanover Square (National Archives PROB 11/652/159); her son Henry Furness was the beneficiary. It is just possible that she was the Elizabeth Corkland, of Winkfield, who married George Furness, of London, by licence, at Old Windsor on 18 September 1693.

[237] Henry Harris and George Furness are recorded together in Charles Street West in the tax on real and personal property in 1694. See the online database *London Lives 1690 to 1800*, www.londonlives.org. The Survey of London, vol. 36, *Covent Garden*, pp. 195–195, records Henry Harris as a ratepayer in Charles Street from c.1687 to c.1702.

[238] See, for example, Peter Holland, *The Ornament of Action: Text and Performance in Restoration Comedy* (Cambridge: Cambridge University Press, 1979).

[239] As listed in the Appendix.

[240] See, for example, Cibber, *Apology*, pp. 77, 102, 120, 143, 312.

the highest' in 1663, there is no sign that Harris entertained comparable ambitions. In fact, neither the scope nor age of his roles changed greatly from the mid-1660s to the end of his acting life. During the later 1670s he created a small number of older characters such as Apemantus in Shadwell's adaptation of *Timon of Athens* (1678), Tiresias in Dryden and Lee's *Oedipus* (1678), and the King in Tate's *The Loyal General* (1679), but warriors and men-about-town continued to feature among his new roles. For him, acting had become one profession among others, a routine that fed the wallet rather than the ego. In the early years of the Duke's Company he had bridled at the notion that an acting career meant a lifetime in middling roles, but he soon consigned himself to that very doom. With 'the King and everybody else crying him up so high, and that above Baterton', he may have flirted with what we now call stardom, but his performing life settled into the less glamorous shape encompassed by another modern term, that of the jobbing actor.

That he was also a jobbing engraver and court official limited his claim to 'celebrity' in a period now widely viewed as cradle to that phenomenon.[241] None of his contemporaries thought to write about his life, as John Downes and Charles Gildon did Betterton's, while few copies have been traced of the mezzotint from Greenhill's portrait. But then we might doubt whether 'celebrity' in the modern sense really existed in the absence of mass media, since there could be few 'illusions of availability' in the tightly packed, rather parochial confines of late seventeenth-century London, where no more than 30,000 people went to the theatre.[242] Harris certainly displayed little sign of the alluring combination of indifference and intimacy which Joseph Roach detects in stardom à-la-Hollywood; indeed, the more Roach and his successors press home resemblances between the management of Restoration theatres and twentieth-century film studios, the greater the differences appear to be.[243] However we might define Harris's fame, there is no evidence that it spread beyond London.

To the extent that the modern term 'celebrity' is appropriate, it may only apply to the evidently fetishized bodies of the first English actresses, whose careers were managed so as to protect theatre managers' interests, obstruct access to other kinds of rewarding work, and prevent them (not always successfully) from being abducted. Their 'illusion of availability' was fuelled partly by false association with the oldest profession and therefore with low social origins. For all his trade background and connections, there is no sign that

---

[241] E.g. in the works by Roach, Meyer Spacks, Fawcett, and Tillyard cited earlier in n.25, 26, 139, 140.

[242] The figure is drawn from Allan Richard Botica's 'Audience, Playhouse and Play in English Restoration Theatre, 1660-1710', Unpublished DPhil thesis, Oxford University, 1985.

[243] E.g. Roach, *It*, p. 177.

Harris was ever accused of rising talent-free from nowhere ('famous for being famous', in modern parlance), unlike the actresses tarred with being, in Deborah C. Payne's words, 'the nouveau aristocrats of an emerging visual culture that rewards a captivating performance'.[244] Harris's social accomplishments were, after all, sufficient to impress people as different as Samuel Pepys and Judge Robert Wiseman, and they appear continuous with the qualities of 'port and mien' John Downes observed in his stage presence.[245] In a patriarchal culture, male charisma might elide lowly origins.

It was the economic culture of Restoration London that best defined Henry Harris's working life. What emerges from his biography is the diversity of interests that in some cases had little to do with the stage, all in order to keep his head above water amid a chaotic marriage. It is sobering to reflect that as far as the records show, acting occupied less than half of his working life; that is, the twenty years between 1661 and 1681, against the nearly fifty between completing his apprenticeship as a scale maker and his last known assignment at The Mint. At the same time, his uneasy relationship with court politics begins to shed light on how actors as well as playwrights had to navigate a fraught period of regime change, and how they, like writers, depended on patronage in challenging times. That he did so via elevated social networks proposes fresh arguments about the social status at least of the more prominent actors.

As for the rest, whether middle-ranker or mere walker-on, the many lives of Henry Harris pose a simpler question. How on earth could they, like so many of their successors down the centuries, make a living at all? To answer that question we need to follow Lear's advice and expose ourselves to feel what wretches felt. In the naked beggar, the King does after all see himself. Put another way, celebrity culture and the gig economy are two sides of the same coin. Without the scores of jobbing and no-jobbing actors who feed them their lines and livelihoods, we would not know what a celebrity actor was. For all his success as an actor and his multiple streams of income, Henry Harris illustrates the entrenched precarity of the acting profession as vividly as any bit-part player. So, when it comes to the history of celebrity, we might learn to broaden our gaze to embrace that murkier crew of grifters who have always been a majority in the profession, and have pursued their craft only because they had, in addition to acting, other business.

---

[244] Deborah C. Payne, 'The Restoration Actress', in J. Douglas Canfield and Deborah C. Payne, eds., *Cultural Readings of Restoration and Eighteenth-Century English Theater* (Athens, GA: University of Georgia Press, 1995), p. 35.

[245] See earlier, n.94.

Abbreviations of Frequently Cited Sources

Boswell: Eleanore Boswell, *The Restoration Court Stage 1660–1702* (Cambridge MA: Harvard University Press, 1932)

Challis, *Mint*: C.E. Challis, *A New History of the Royal Mint* (Cambridge: Cambridge University Press, 1992)

Cibber: Colley Cibber, *An Apology for the Life of Mr Colley Cibber, Comedian and Late Patentee of the Theatre Royal,* ed. David Roberts (Cambridge: Cambridge University Press, 2022)

CSPD: *Calendar of State Papers, Domestic Series, of the Reign of Charles II,* ed. Mary Anne Everett Green et al (London: Longmans, Eyre & Spottiswood, Mackie & Co, HMSO, 1866–1934)

Document Register: *A Register of English Theatrical Documents, 1660–1737.* 2 vols, ed. Judith Milhous and Robert D. Hume (Carbondale & Edwardsville: Southern Illinois University Press, 1991)

Downes: John Downes, *Roscius Anglicanus,* ed. Judith Milhous and Robert D. Hume (London: Society for Theatre Research, 1987)

LS1: *The London Stage. Part 1: 1660–1700,* ed. William van Lennep (Carbondale: Southern Illinois University Press, 1963)

Nicoll: Allardyce Nicoll, *Restoration Drama 1660–1700,* 3rd ed. (Cambridge: Cambridge University Press, 1939)

Pepys, *Diary*: Samuel Pepys, *The Diary of Samuel Pepys,* ed. Robert Latham and William Matthews (London: Bell & Hyman, 1971–83)

Appendix
A Checklist of Henry Harris's Known Roles

Role	Playwright and play	First known performance
Alphonso	William Davenant, *The Siege of Rhodes*	28 June 1661
Young Palatine	William Davenant, *The Wits*	15 August 1661
Horatio	William Shakespeare, *Hamlet*	24 August 1661
Sir Andrew Aguecheek	William Shakespeare, *Twelfth Night*	11 September 1661
Prince Prospero	William Davenant, *Love and Honour*	21 October 1661
Young Trueman	Abraham Cowley, *The Cutter of Coleman Street*	16 December 1661
Romeo	William Shakespeare, *Romeo and Juliet*	1 March 1662
Ferdinand	John Webster, *The Duchess of Malfi*	30 September 1662
Beaupré	Thomas Porter, *The Villain*	18 October 1662
Antonio	Samuel Tuke, *The Adventures of Five Hours*	8 January 1663
Salerno	Robert Stapylton, *The Slighted Maid*	23 February 1663
Cardinal Wolsey	William Shakespeare/John Fletcher, *Henry VIII*	22 December 1663
Sir Frederick Frollick	George Etherege, *The Comical Revenge*	March 1664
Not known	George Digby, *Worse and Worse*	20 July 1664
King Henry	Roger Boyle, Earl of Orrery, *Henry V*	13 August 1664
Theocles	William Davenant, *The Rivals*	10 September 1664
Macduff	William Shakespeare/William Davenant, *Macbeth*	5 November 1664
Mustapha	Roger Boyle, Earl of Orrery, *Mustapha*	3 April 1665
Cardinal	James Shirley, *The Cardinal*	February 1667
Richmond	John Caryll, *The English Princess*	7 March 1667
Warner	John Dryden, *Feign'd Innocence*	15 August 1667

(cont.)

Role	Playwright and play	First known performance
Ferdinand	William Shakespeare/William Davenant, *The Tempest*	7 November 1667
Sir Joslin	George Etherege, *She Would if She Could*	6 February 1668
Don John	William Davenant, *The Man's the Master*	26 March 1668
Sir Positive At-All	Thomas Shadwell, *The Sullen Lovers*	2 May 1668
Not known	Thomas Shadwell, *The Royal Shepherdess*	25 February 1669
Appius	John Webster/Thomas Betterton, *The Roman Virgin*	12 May 1669
Peregrine Woodland	John Caryll, *Sir Salomon*	April 1670
Tysamnes	Edward Howard, *The Woman's Conquest*	November 1670
Prexaspes	Elkanah Settle, *Cambyses*	10 January 1671
Sir Franckman	Edward Howard, *The Six Days' Adventure*	6 March 1671
Cardinal	John Crowne, *Juliana*	June 1671
Ferdinand	John Crowne, *Charles VIII*	November 1671
Trickmore	Edward Ravenscroft, *The Citizen Turn'd Gentleman*	4 July 1672
Not known	Henry Payne, *The Fatal Jealousie*	3 August 1672
Merry	Henry Payne, *The Morning Ramble*	4 November 1672
Rains	Thomas Shadwell, *Epsom Wells*	2 December 1672
Antonio	Joseph Arrowsmith, *The Reformation*	May 1673
Muly Labas	Elkanah Settle, *The Empress of Morocco*	3 July 1673
Zungteus	Elkanah Settle, *The Conquest of China by the Tartars*	28 May 1675
Theramnes	Thomas Otway, *Alcibiades*	September 1675
Merry	John Crowne, *The Country Wit*	10 January 1676
Ulama	Elkanah Settle, *Ibrahim the Illustrious Bassa*	March 1676
Medley	George Etherege, *The Man of Mode*	11 March 1676

(cont.)

Role	Playwright and play	First known performance
Don John	Otway, *Don Carlos*	8 June 1676
Ferdinand	Aphra Behn, *Abdelazer*	3 July 1676
Don Gusmun	Edward Ravenscroft, *The Wrangling Lovers*	25 July 1676
Mecaenas	Charles Sedley, *Antony and Cleopatra*	12 February 1677
Thoas	Charles Davenant, *Circe*	12 May 1677
Ranger	Thomas Durfey, *A Fond Husband*	31 May 1677
Cassander	Samuel Pordage, *The Siege of Babylon*	September 1677
Apemantus	William Shakespeare/Thomas Shadwell, *Timon of Athens*	January 1678
Valentine	Thomas Otway, *Friendship in Fashion*	5 April 1678
Antonio	John Leanerd, *The Counterfeits*	28 May 1678
Tiresias	John Dryden/Nathaniel Lee, *Oedipus*	September 1678
Hector	John Banks, *The Destruction of Troy*	November 1678
Ulysses	John Dryden, *Troilus and Cressida*	April 1679
Beverly	Thomas Durfey, *The Virtuous Wife*	September 1679
The King	Nahum Tate, *The Loyal General*	December 1679
Cardinal	John Crowne, *Henry VI*	April 1681

Bibliography

Addison, Joseph, *The Spectator* no.288 (30 January 1712).

Anderson, James, *A Genealogical History of the House of Yvery*, 2 vols (London: H. Woodfall, 1742).

Aston, Anthony, *A Brief Supplement to Colley Cibber Esq. His Lives of the Famous Actors and Actresses* (London: Anthony Aston, 1747).

Backscheider, Paula, 'Beyond City Walls: Restoration Actors in the Drapers' Company', *Theatre Survey* 45.1 (May 2004), 75–87.

Baxter, Richard, *Reliquiae Baxterianae*, 3 vols (London, 1696).

Boswell, Eleanore, *The Restoration Court Stage* (Cambridge, MA: Harvard University Press, T. Parkhurst et al., 1932).

Calendar of State Papers, Domestic Series, of the Reign of Charles II, Mary Anne Everett Green (ed.) (London: Longmans, Eyre & Spottiswood, Mackie, HMSO, 1866–1934).

Calendar of State Papers, Colonial, America and West Indies, 1669–1674, ed. W. Noel Sainsbury (London: HMSO, 1889).

Calendar of Treasury Books, 1685–1689, ed. William A. Shaw (London: HMSO, 1923).

Caryll, John, *Sir Salomon; Or, The Cautious Coxcomb* (London: Henry Herringman, 1671).

Challis, Christopher E., *A New History of the Royal Mint* (Cambridge: Cambridge University Press, 1992).

  'Henry Harris', in *Oxford Dictionary of National Biography*, ed. Lawrence Goldmann, 60 vols, pp. 427–428 (Oxford: Oxford University Press, XXV.427–428).

Chambers, Edmund K., *The Elizabethan Stage*, 4 vols (Oxford: Clarendon Press, 1923).

Crowne, John, *The Countrey Wit* (London: James Magnes and Richard Bentley, 1675).

  Henry the Sixth with the Murder of Humphrey, Duke of Gloucester (London: R. Bentley and M. Magnes, 1681).

Cibber, Colley, *An Apology for the Life of Mr Colley Cibber, Comedian and Late Patentee of the Theatre Royal*, ed. David Roberts (Cambridge: Cambridge University Press, 2022).

Dale, Thomas C., *The Inhabitants of London in 1638* (London: Society of Genealogists, 1931).

Davenant, Sir William, *The Siege of Rhodes* (London: Henry Herringman, 1663).

The Wits (London: Bedel and Collins, 1665).

The Works of Sir William Davenant (London: Henry Herringman, 1973).

Downes, John, *Roscius Anglicanus*, ed. Judith Milhous and Robert D. Hume (London: Society for Theatre Research, 1987).

Etherege, Sir George, *The Comical Revenge; or, Love in a Tub* (London: Henry Herringman, 1664).

The Plays of Sir George Etherege, ed. Michael Cordner (Cambridge: Cambridge University Press, 1982).

Favin, André, *The Theatre of Honour and Knighthood* (London: William Jaggard, 1623).

Ferdinand, Christine, 'Thomas Betterton's Book-Trade Apprenticeship and the Amazing Careers of His Two Masters, John Holden and John Rhodes, with Some Notes on the Actor's Library', *The Library: The Transactions of the Bibliographical Society* 23.4 (December 2022), 435–57.

'Commodities and the Acting Profession: A Newly Discovered Inventory for William and Susanna Mountfort's "India Shop" (1692)', *Huntington Library Quarterly* 86.1 (Spring 2023), 73–109.

Halliwell-Phillips, James O., *A Collection of Ancient Documents respecting the Office of the Master of the Revels* (London: T. Richards, 1870).

Herbert, William, *The History of the Twelve Great Livery Companies of London*, 2 vols (London: William Herbert, 1836–7).

Hill, Tracey, *Pageantry and Power: A Cultural History of the Early Modern Lord Mayor's Show, 1585–1639* (Manchester: Manchester University Press, 2010).

Hooke, Jacob, *Pinacotheca Bettertonaeana: The Library of a Seventeenth-Century Actor*, ed. David Roberts (London: Society for Theatre Research, 2013).

Howe, Elizabeth, *The First English Actresses* (Cambridge: Cambridge University Press, 1992).

Hughes, Derek, *English Drama 1660–1700* (Oxford: Clarendon Press, 1996).

Hume, Robert D., 'Theatre History, 1660–1800: Aims, Materials, Methodology', in Michael Cordner and Peter Holland, eds., *Players, Playwrights, Playhouses: Investigating Performance, 1660–1800* (Basingstoke: Palgrave Macmillan, 2007), pp. 9–44.

'The Value of Money in Eighteenth-Century England: Incomes, Prices, Buying Power – and Some Problems in Cultural Economics', *Huntington Library Quarterly* 77.4 (Winter 2014), 373–416.

Jacobsen, Helen, 'Luxury Consumption, Cultural Politics, and the Career of the Earl of Arlington, 1660-1685', *The Historical Journal* 52.2 (June 2009), 295–317.

Kathman, David, 'Grocers, Goldsmiths and Drapers: Freemen and Apprentices in the Elizabethan Theatre', *Shakespeare Quarterly* 55.1 (2004), 1–49.

Malcolm, Alistair, 'Pretending to Be Catholic? Sir Henry Bennet, the Alliance with Spain and Stuart Dalliance with Rome, 1656-62', in Robin Eagles and Coleman A. Dennehy, eds., *Henry Bennet, Earl of Arlington, and his World: Restoration Court, Politics and Diplomacy* (London: Routledge, 2021) pp. 31–51.

Milhous, Judith, *Thomas Betterton and the Management of Lincoln's Inn Fields, 1695–1708* (Carbondale: Southern Illinois University Press, 1987).

'Thomas Betterton', *Oxford Dictionary of National Biography*, ed. Lawrence Goldmann, 60 vols (Oxford: Oxford University Press, 2004), V.558–9.

Milhous, Judith, and Robert D. Hume, eds., *A Register of English Theatrical Documents, 1660–1737*. 2 vols (Carbondale: Southern Illinois University Press, 1991).

The Publication of Plays in London 1660–1800: Playwrights, Publishers and the Market (London: British Library, 2015).

Nelken, Rachel, 'Portfolio Careers in the Arts: One Part Pain, Two Parts Pleasure', *The Guardian*, 5 March 2013.

Nicoll, Allardyce, *Restoration Drama 1660–1700*, 3rd ed. (Cambridge: Cambridge University Press, 1939).

Ollard, Richard, *Pepys: A Biography* (Oxford: Oxford University Press, 1984)

Palmer, Richard, 'In the Court of Arches: The Private Life of John Lacy, Restoration Actor', *Archives* LVIII.1 (2023), 1–13.

and David Roberts, 'Harris vs Harris: A Restoration Actor at the Court of Arches', *Huntington Library Quarterly* 87.3 (Autumn 2024), pp. 483–500.

Parker, George, *The True News; Or, Mercurius Anglicanus* (London: George Parker), 4–7 February 1680.

Pepys, Samuel, *The Diary of Samuel Pepys*, ed. Robert Latham and William Matthews (London: Bell & Hyman, 1971–83).

Probert, Rebecca, *Marriage Law and Practice in the Long Eighteenth Century: A Reassessment* (Cambridge: Cambridge University Press, 2009).

Rawlins, Thomas, *The Rebellion: A Tragedy* (London: Daniel Frere, 1640).

Roberts, David, *Thomas Betterton: The Greatest Actor of the Restoration Stage* (Cambridge: Cambridge University Press, 2010).

'Writing the Ethical Life: Theatrical Biography and the Case of Thomas Betterton', in Claire Cochrane and Jo Robinson, eds., *Theatre History and*

Historiography. Ethics, Evidence and Truth (Basingstoke: Palgrave Macmillan, 2016), pp. 33–47.

Rowell, George, and Anthony Jackson, *The Repertory Movement: A History of Regional Theatre in Britain* (Cambridge: Cambridge University Press, 1984).

Schama, Simon, *Landscape and Memory* (London: Harper Collins, 1995).

Segar, William, *Honour Military and Civill Contained in Four Books* (London: Robert Barker, 1602).

Selden, John, *The Duello or Single Combat from antiquity* (London: John Helme, 1610).

Settle, Elkanah, 'To the Honourable Company of Clothworkers', in *The Triumphs of London Prepared for the Entertainment of the Right Honourable Sir Thomas Lane* (London: Richard Baldwin, 1694).

Shakespeare, William, *Twelfth Night; Or, What You Will*, ed. J. M. Lothian and T. W. Craik (London: Methuen, 1975).

—— and John Fletcher, *King Henry VIII*, ed. John Margeson (Cambridge: Cambridge University Press, 1990).

Stapylton, Robert, *The Slighted Maid* (London: Thomas Dring, 1663).

Stockdale, Eric, 'Sir John Kelynge, Chief Justice of the King's Bench 1665-1671', Bedfordshire Historical Records Society 59 (1980), 43–53.

Tatham, John, *London's Triumph* (London: H. Brown, 1662).

Thomas, David, and Arnold Hare, eds., *Restoration and Georgian England 1660–1800* (Cambridge: Cambridge University Press, 1989).

Towers, Joseph, 'The Life of Dr John Radcliffe', *British Biography*, 10 vols (Sherborne, 1766–7), VII.256–7.

Tuke, Sir Samuel, *The Adventures of Five Hours* (London: Henry Herringman, 1663).

van Lennep, William, ed., *The London Stage. Part 1: 1660–1700* (Carbondale: Southern Illinois University Press, 1963).

Wanko, Cheryl, *Roles of Authority: Thespian Biography and Celebrity in Eighteenth-Century Britain* (Lubbock: Texas Tech University Press, 2003).

Williams, Oliver E., Lucas Lacasa, and Vito Latora, 'Quantifying and predicting success in show business', *Nature Communications* 10, article no. 2256 (2019).

Winn, James A., *John Dryden and His World* (New Haven: Yale University Press, 1987).

Web Sources

British History: www.british-history.ac.uk

Acknowledgements

My thanks to Bethany Thomas at CUP for suggesting Elements as an outlet for this project, and to the series editors, Professors Markman Ellis and Eve Tavor Bannet. I've benefitted from presenting a digest of the project to colleagues at the Royal Birmingham Conservatoire, under the watchful eye of Professor Sasha Dundjerovic. Dr Izabela Hopkins has assisted with bibliographic searches. The advice of the Press's two anonymous readers has been extremely helpful. Finally, I could not have contemplated this project if I had not been contacted out of the blue by Richard Palmer, formerly Librarian at Lambeth Palace, about his discoveries in the records of the Court of Arches.

Cambridge Elements

Eighteenth-Century Connections

Series Editors
Eve Tavor Bannet
University of Oklahoma

Eve Tavor Bannet is George Lynn Cross Professor Emeritus, University of Oklahoma and editor of *Studies in Eighteenth-Century Culture*. Her monographs include *Empire of Letters: Letter Manuals and Transatlantic Correspondence 1688–1820* (Cambridge, 2005), *Transatlantic Stories and the History of Reading, 1720–1820* (Cambridge, 2011), and *Eighteenth-Century Manners of Reading: Print Culture and Popular Instruction in the Anglophone Atlantic World* (Cambridge, 2017). She is editor of *British and American Letter Manuals 1680–1810* (Pickering & Chatto, 2008), *Emma Corbett* (Broadview, 2011) and, with Susan Manning, *Transatlantic Literary Studies* (Cambridge, 2012).

Markman Ellis
Queen Mary University of London

Markman Ellis is Professor of Eighteenth-Century Studies at Queen Mary University of London. He is the author of *The Politics of Sensibility: Race, Gender and Commerce in the Sentimental Novel* (1996), *The History of Gothic Fiction* (2000), *The Coffee-House: a Cultural History* (2004), and *Empire of Tea* (co-authored, 2015). He edited *Eighteenth-Century Coffee-House Culture* (4 vols, 2006) and *Tea and the Tea-Table in Eighteenth-Century England* (4 vols 2010), and co-editor of *Discourses of Slavery and Abolition* (2004) and *Prostitution and Eighteenth-Century Culture: Sex, Commerce and Morality* (2012).

Advisory Board
Linda Bree, *Independent*
Claire Connolly, *University College Cork*
Gillian Dow, *University of Southampton*
James Harris, *University of St Andrews*
Thomas Keymer, *University of Toronto*
Jon Mee, *University of York*
Carla Mulford, *Penn State University*
Nicola Parsons, *University of Sydney*
Manushag Powell, *Purdue University*
Robbie Richardson, *University of Kent*
Shef Rogers, *University of Otago*
Eleanor Shevlin, *West Chester University*
David Taylor, *Oxford University*
Chloe Wigston Smith, *University of York*
Roxann Wheeler, *Ohio State University*
Eugenia Zuroski, *MacMaster University*

About the Series
Exploring connections between verbal and visual texts and the people, networks, cultures and places that engendered and enjoyed them during the long Eighteenth Century, this innovative series also examines the period's uses of oral, written and visual media, and experiments with the digital platform to facilitate communication of original scholarship with both colleagues and students.

Cambridge Elements

Eighteenth-Century Connections

Elements in the Series

Pastoral Care through Letters in the British Atlantic
Alison Searle

The Domino and the Eighteenth-Century London Masquerade: A Social Biography of a Costume
Meghan Kobza

Paratext Printed with New English Plays, 1660–1700
Robert D. Hume

The Art of the Actress
Fashioning Identities

A Performance History of The Fair Penitent
Elaine McGirr

Labour of the Stitch: The Making and Remaking of Fashionable Georgian Dress
Serena Dyer

Early English Periodicals and Early Modern Social Media
Margaret J. M. Ezell

Reading with the Burneys: Patronage, Paratext, and Performance
Sophie Coulombeau

On Wonder
Tita Chico

The Epistemologies of Progress
Richard Adelman

Networks of Reception in the Eighteenth-Century British Press and Laurence Sterne
Mary Newbould

Restoration Acting and Other Business: The Lives of Henry Harris
David Roberts

A full series listing is available at: www.cambridge.org/EECC

For EU product safety concerns, contact us at Calle de José Abascal, 56–1°, 28003 Madrid, Spain or eugpsr@cambridge.org.

www.ingramcontent.com/pod-product-compliance
Lightning Source LLC
LaVergne TN
LVHW011856060526
838200LV00054B/4370